ANCHORED

IN FREEDOM

Messages of Truth that Bring Hope

NICOLE MOORE

DYNAMIC
HARVEST MEDIA

ANCHORED IN FREEDOM
© 2020 Nicole Moore

Unless otherwise noted, Scripture quotations are taken from the New King James Version®. Copyright © 1982 by Thomas Nelson, Inc. Used by permission. All rights reserved.

Scriptures quotations marked (NIV) taken from the New International Version®. Copyright © 1973, 1978, 1984, 2011 by Biblica, Inc.™ Used by permission of Zondervan. All rights reserved worldwide. www.zondervan.com.

Cover design: Daryl Oldenburg, ISI Media

Photo credits: Andrew Moore, Pixabay.com, Unsplash.com

ISBN: 978-1-7346537-0-0

anchoredinfreedom.com

DYNAMIC
HARVEST MEDIA

ENDORSEMENTS

Anchored in Freedom is for people looking for simple solutions to everyday problems. It will grow your faith and trust in the heart of the Lord. At the same time, it will remove the shackles of wrong thinking. It's all about the freedom to love and be loved by the Father! Nicole has been so transparent and it shines through in this amazing book. A must read.

Troy and Leanna Brewer
Founders and Pastors, OpenDoor Church
Troy Brewer Ministries
S.P.A.R.K. Worldwide
Authors

Nicole has written a book about something we all want - hope! I don't know a single person who doesn't want it in their life, and yet, our culture is desperately grabbing scraps of counterfeit hope only to end up disappointed and empty handed. Inspired by her own life story, Nicole has beautifully put the process on paper of how any of us can courageously shift from placing our hope in false support to placing it all on Jesus - the only hope that won't disappoint!

Jenny Donnelly
Founder, Her Voice Movement
Co-Founder, Tetelestai Ministries
Author, Still: Seven Ways to Find Calm in the Chaos

Dedication

For Kevin, Andrew and Jade

I love our adventures together!

I love you and am so thankful for you.

ACKNOWLEDGMENTS

Writing this book has been an incredibly challenging and extremely rewarding process. I could not have done it alone. God created us to need one another and writing a book definitely revealed that truth to me!

Jesus, thank you for helping me find the freedom to be "me!"

Kevin, thank you for giving me the "place" to do this. I needed you to be understanding, supportive and a foundation to keep me stable and you came through for me in all of these ways! Thank you for being patient with me all of these years while I discovered just how free I could be. I am still learning and I am thankful for you!

Andrew and Jade, thank you for being understanding of the time it took to put this together. I know it wasn't just the time of actually writing this book. You have both been so understanding of every position the Lord has put me in so that I could learn these truths. I pray that my understanding of freedom is your starting point and you guys lead the way — beyond what I could ever imagine. You are both world changers. I am so thankful to be your mom!

Mom and Dad, thank you for teaching me to see the best in people —including me! I am so thankful for parents that believe in me the way you do! Thank you!

Pastor Troy and Pastor Leanna, you have opened my mind to a whole new way of living in freedom and I am so thankful for your example!

Kyp Shillam, thank you for editing my wordy chapters. You gave me hope when I needed it!

Carol Martinez, thank you for being such an encourager and creating such a beautiful book layout!

Daryl Oldenburg, thank you for a beautiful cover and your patience in the process!

Thank you to all of my family, friends, acquaintances, and mentors that I may have never met. Each of you has influenced my journey and I am thankful for you.

TABLE OF CONTENTS

INTRODUCTION

Honestly, I don't always read the introductions to books. I just want to get into the chapters! Thank you for reading this one. My name, Nicole, means "victory of the people." Finding victory and freedom are the driving forces behind so much of what I do. It's been a journey to find my own freedom and I am still in the process. I have a passion to share my victories with others so they can use the same strategies to find freedom, or at least be encouraged that it is possible. That's what love does. Love has compassion but also helps us up! I also believe in being transparent – my journey involves ups and downs.

Just recently, I realized writing a book is very much like living with an autoimmune disease. I was diagnosed with MS a while back. It's a struggle that isn't always obvious to everyone else. After many years of strange symptoms, I finally learned there was a reason. MS is not my identity. I don't say "I have it" because it is not mine and it is on its way out! Jesus is my healer and I fully believe I already have complete healing and ALL symptoms will stop. Until then, there are symptoms no one else can see that cause great struggle for me. One of them is limited fine motor skills, which is why I "stamp" my books rather than sign them. I could list all the health struggles I face but that's no fun! It's also not where my focus is.

Funny how no one told me life doesn't stop just because you are writing a book. I still had to juggle laundry, kids, coordinating conferences, making meals, getting a new dog and EVERYTHING else WHILE I was writing. I looked fine on the outside, but on the inside I was screaming, "I just want to finish this chapter!" Philippians 4:13 became very real for me – especially the ALL things part!

Don't we all carry things beneath the surface others can't see? Some of those things drain the energy you need to find victory. There are also "good" things beneath the surface that may be covered up by hurt, fear, or wrong thinking. Freedom is the answer! Jesus died and rose again to give you a place in His family, which comes with incredible benefits. Freedom is one of those benefits and it already belongs to you. *Anchored in Freedom* doesn't make sense in the natural but it makes complete sense in our spiritual lives. An anchor keeps you where you need to be. We need to be anchored in the truth that makes us free. I pray you find that truth in EVERY chapter.

The goal of this book is to start a conversation between you and the Lord. If you finish a chapter and think, "She should've said…" or, "What about…?" and you are stirred to find out more, I have done my job. How deep you go is up to you! These truths don't work well without a relationship with Jesus. Trying to change yourself in your own strength will eventually lead to a dead end filled with frustration. On the other hand, inviting Him into your heart and following His lead will take you to levels of freedom that seem too good to be true. The Lord loves you perfectly just the way you are! When you choose Jesus, He chooses you forever. We seek victory and freedom *because* we are loved, not to earn His love. Be patient with yourself because He is! I want to help open up the world of hearing Him in everyday life and joining Him in the journey toward the freedom He has already given you. Enjoy the process. He's in every moment of it.

Praying for you!

Nicole

1

ANCHORED

For years, I have said, "I am going to put an anchor in that!" By this, I mean I would commit to something even though I had no idea how I was going to make it happen. If I knew it was something I should do, I also knew I would figure out a way later!

Or, maybe I would publicize a goal to create accountability to get it done. In fact, just to write this book I had to put some anchors out there! I reached out to the graphic designer and editor that I wanted to use before I even had time to make it happen! Now, as I write this, they are waiting on me. Sometimes, I hate that, but in this case it's good. It's an anchor that will lead me into the place the Lord wants me to be.

Recently, I started seeing anchors everywhere! Hats, bags, shirts, and so many tattoos! You have no idea how many people have anchor tattoos. Start paying attention and you will see them all over the place. I knew God was trying to get my attention and when I listened, He kept talking.

God wants us to really "know" this truth. He doesn't want us to have a casual surface "knowing."

Have you ever been to karaoke? If not, here's how it usually works: The D.J. has a book of hundreds of songs. You look through the book and choose one you want to sing, then he puts you on the list of singers. I don't always know the titles of the songs. So, people usually flip through and find one they feel like they know pretty well.

You might say, "Yeah, yeah. I know that one. I'll do that one!" Then, it's your turn to get on the stage with a microphone in your hand in front of everyone to sing. The lyrics come up on the screen in front of you and the colored words show you what you should be singing. It's then you realize, "Wait, I don't remember this part." You have no idea how to sing the "oohs" and "aahs." You don't really know the timing, so you're behind and all of the words get jumbled up. What happens is you realize that without someone to sing along with, you don't know the song as well as you thought you did. You aren't ready to sing it by yourself, especially not in front of people.

Then there are songs you know from beginning to end without the music. You know the timing perfectly and you feel the beat in your soul. You can sing the ohhs, aahs, and both the girl and the guy's parts. You KNOW this song! It's in your heart – you know it.

That is the kind of "knowing" God wants us to have about hope.

The Word says this about hope:

We have this hope as an anchor for the soul, firm and secure. It enters the inner sanctuary behind the curtain, where our forerunner, Jesus, has entered on our behalf. – **Hebrews 6:19-20 (NIV)**

The anchor represents our hope. What does an anchor do? It keeps us from being swept away in the wrong direction and being tossed to and fro.

What Is Hope?

It's important to know what hope is. In our society, we use words incorrectly all the time. For example, when someone apologizes for hurting us we are taught to respond by saying, "It's okay." No. It's not! It's totally not okay that they hurt us. If it were okay, we wouldn't mind them doing it again! Our response should be, "I forgive you."

So, let's start with what hope is *not*. It's not a wish. People say, "I hope that happens" or "I hope I get this for Christmas." That leaves us holding our breath wondering what will really happen.

God's definition of hope is this: a confident expectation of what is to come.

We know this is God's definition of *hope* because the Word says in Titus 1:2 that we have hope in eternal life. I'm not wishing I have eternal life. I'm hoping – putting my confident expectation – in the fact it will happen and that eternal life is God's promise to me. There are so many other scriptures about hope in the Bible. Do a word study and you will see that EVERY time hope is written, the words "confident expectation," not wish, can be substituted for the word hope.

As we use the anchor to represent our hope, we have to remember the anchor is only as good as what it is anchored to. If we have a good solid anchor but we put it in Jell-o, we will quickly find out the anchor will not hold.

As Christians, our anchor is in the Lord – behind the veil – not just on the edge of who He is where we hope the angle is just right so it doesn't slip. We are anchored in Him – in the secret place!

Even as Christians, we are tempted to put our hope in something other than the Lord. The truth is, sometimes we don't even realize we have misplaced our anchor until there's a little tension applied and you realize that your anchor, your hope, was not as secure as you thought it was. The anchor gets tugged on, becomes loose and you end up being tossed through the waves rather than remaining secure and stable in the Lord.

It's important to STOP right here and remember:

There is therefore now no condemnation to those who are in Christ Jesus, who do not walk according to the flesh, but according to the Spirit. – Romans 8:1

Anytime we are growing in Christ by evaluating our lives to see how we can better line up with truth, there is a tendency to feel very disappointed in our own choices. It's easy to feel the heaviness of everything we've done wrong and it can create a hopelessness in our hearts. Always remember you are made righteous and whole by Christ's sacrifice. Nothing more and nothing less. You cannot be good enough to receive His righteousness. God sees you as righteous because of His Son. His love for you is constant and pure in every way. He loves you the same on days when you get everything done on your checklist and treat everyone nicely, as He does on the days you cannot get out of your house because you're afraid you'll beat somebody up.

Of course, the Lord wants us to pursue victory in every place in our lives while we are here on this earth. It brings Him glory and it helps us avoid trouble. When we walk in freedom, we are able to fulfill our kingdom purpose here on earth. No one has arrived. It's a process and we need to learn to give grace to ourselves and others. Please don't listen to the voice of condemnation that says, "It's hopeless. You've messed up too much. You should be ashamed. Don't tell anyone what you've done or they won't love you anymore. God can never forgive you." That voice is a liar!

> *"I can't afford to have thoughts in my head about me that God doesn't have in His."* — Bill Johnson

Receive His truth and receive His freedom. As we jump in to find victory, remember to give yourself grace just as God does.

There are so many places we could potentially place our anchor (hope). Let's look at just a few:

1. Financial Status or Possessions

Suddenly losing your job or getting an unexpected bill can certainly make you evaluate your hope. These are difficult circumstances to deal with. Sometimes, it doesn't even take something so extreme to get our attention. For ladies, perhaps you don't have the money to get your nails done like you always have, or you have to wear the "same" dress again to a party instead of buying a new one. For guys, maybe you can't go hunting this year like you have for last five years and your friend just got a new car, but you can barely afford to put gas in yours. The enemy likes to use those times when you're feeling like everybody else is able to have something, but you are not. These are the times when you realize your hope was in those things to make you happy and secure. It's TRUE that you need the money to pay the bill, eat, buy your kid's shoes and put gas in the car. Your reaction to the times when it appears you don't have enough reveals where your anchor rests. Is your hope in *having* enough or knowing the One who *is* enough?

It's not wrong to have financial success – just don't put your hope in it! King Solomon had tons of wealth and in the end, he realized his wealth did not satisfy. When you put your hope/anchor in your financial status it does not hold. You can fall into this temptation whether you have a lot or a little.

The Word doesn't give us great detail, but I bet Paul had a lot more wealth and material possessions when he was Saul than when he was Paul. He found his Hope was truly in the Lord and the true riches in this world were found when he placed his anchor of Hope in the Lord.

2. Comforts of Life

You may not realize you've put your hope in something besides the Lord until tension reveals it and your anchor does not hold.

People, me included, can turn into animals sometimes if they don't get enough likes on their Facebook post, they have to change their plans because of someone else, they have to do something out of their comfort zone, or their expectations are not met.

Sometimes, we think we have great hope and faith, but in reality, it's only because we are staying in our comfort zone and not allowing God to move outside of it. It is much easier to look like the perfect Christian that is confident and secure when everything is comfortable around us. Truly being anchored in the Lord creates a different comfort zone that is secure in Him!

Years ago, I was asked to sing at a friend's wedding. The guy was a millionaire and it was a very fancy and expensive event at a country club. As I was waiting to go out onto the patio to sing, I was standing next to the pastor when the wedding coordinator looked out the window and said a very bad word. We soon found out it was because a plant was out of place. She rushed out to fix the plant and I looked at the pastor and said, "You know, sometimes I think God lets things like that happen just to remind us that it's really not that big a deal." Then I walked out onto the patio in front of hundreds of people and the soundman began to play the music. Well, I thought it was my song and then I realized it was not. He started playing the wrong song. I said, "That's not it." Then he played another song and it was still not the right one. The third time it was finally the right song, so I began to sing.

Somewhere in the middle of the song, I realized I heard another voice. I don't know why I did it, but I stopped singing! He had played the demo track which meant it had a guide voice on it. At that point, everyone in the audience had their mouth open thinking that I had been lip-synching the entire time. I just kept singing and finished the song. I decided right then and there that I wasn't going to tell the bride and groom what had happened and they could find out on the wedding video!

God showed me that a prefect performance wasn't that important. My comfort zone had been increased, my plans had changed because of someone else's mistake, and my expectations were certainly not met! I learned a lot that day.

My wedding story was an easy way to learn. Paul spent much of his life as a Christian in prison. That surely wasn't comfortable. I'm not wishing prison on anybody, but if Paul can find joy in prison, that shows us that his anchor was truly in the Lord. His hope was only in the Lord.

It's not wrong to have comforts–just don't put your hope in them!

3. Ourselves

This is a sneaky one. It can hide behind responsibility, good stewardship, faithfulness or confidence. This is where the sword of the spirit is so valuable. God will help you be completely honest with yourself to find out the places where you are depending on yourself instead of Him. Hear me right, it's not that we don't partner with the Lord in finding victory. That is absolutely His plan for all of us. He just wants us to remember we are partnering *with* Him, that our strength comes from Him and flows through us to accomplish the works He has giving us to do in our lives.

When we try to accomplish something on our own, even if it's for God, it is considered dead works in His eyes. Those dead works leave us feeling empty and frustrated. A friend of mine, Jedidiah, said something that completely changed my perspective about so many things. He wasn't even talking to me when he said this, but I grabbed hold of it instantly. He said, "God wants us to be 100 percent mature and 100 percent dependent at the same time." That doesn't make sense in the natural world. Mature people grow up and become independent. I don't feed my 16-year-old with a spoon or brush my 11-year-old's teeth!

It's different with our Heavenly Father. He wants us to grow and mature, but constantly abide in Him. He wants us to understand that everything in our lives should flow from Him through us and to us. There should not be any part of your life where you are struggling to accomplish things, deal with things, or even see things on your own *without* Him. He should become the lens through which you see everything including yourself. As I said before, many times we don't realize we have an anchor somewhere until tension is applied. For me, the tension comes when I make a mistake.

When I mess up do I beat myself up thinking I have blown it all? When other people see my mistakes do I become fearful that I am not perfect in their eyes and they will look down on me? Do I look at my problems and instantly think of everything I need to do to fix them? Again, it's not that God won't lead me in ways to partner *with* Him to fix things and accomplish things in life. He wants me to abide in Him while being mature and independent at the same time. That comes from trusting Him and knowing He is a good Dad. Knowing He will provide everything I need. Knowing His love for me is absolutely perfect and I don't have to earn it. I can rest in Him. I can be responsible but let that responsibility be out of the overflow of my relationship with Him – not in self-effort to obtain perfection or status in the eyes of others. It's okay to be responsible, a good steward, and confident – just don't put your anchor in it!

4. Jesus

I have learned to be content whatever the circumstances. I know what it is to be in need, and I know what it is to have plenty. I have learned the secret of being content in any and every situation, whether well-fed or hungry, whether living in plenty or in want. I can do all this through him who gives me strength.– Philippians 4:11-13

If we follow Paul's example and put our anchor – our hope – in the Lord, the rock and the foundation of our being, we will not be shaken. We will not be tossed to and fro.

The LORD is my rock and my fortress and my deliverer;
My God, my strength, in whom I will trust;
My shield and the horn of my salvation, my stronghold.
 – Psalm 18:2

We can be stable even in the midst of not having or having financial security; of not having or having comforts of life. Why? Because our hope is in Him.

I'm not saying you won't experience emotions or that God doesn't want you to experience emotions. I'm saying we will not be devastated when we experience the troubles of this world that Jesus said we would face. He never promised an easy life. He did promise that we could be secure in Him no matter what.

"I have told you these things, so that in me you may have peace. In this world you will have trouble. But take heart! I have overcome the world." – John 16:33 (NIV)

The fruit of the spirit is available to us all of the time if we abide in Him. They are not conditional upon our circumstances. You can love in the midst of hurt, you can have peace in the midst of chaos, you can have joy in times of uncertainty. The fruit of the Spirit is ALWAYS available to you!

If you put your anchor of hope in the Lord, and only in the Lord, when tension comes into your life it reveals that you are grounded in your faith and you are secure in Him. Your anchor is in the Rock – not Jell-o!

Earlier I told you I used to say that I was going to "put an anchor out there," meaning that if I put an anchor in something I would be led to where I was supposed to go.

When you read this scripture doesn't it say that?

We have this hope as an anchor for the soul, firm and secure. It enters the inner sanctuary behind the curtain, where our forerunner, Jesus, has entered on our behalf.
– Hebrews 6:19-20

Doesn't the Word tell us our anchor of hope is in Him? The anchor is not to keep us where we are. That is not the Kingdom. The Kingdom of God is progressive.

The anchor is in Him. Its purpose is to draw us into our true identity in Christ.

When our anchor of hope is secure in Him, we have a lifeline that will keep us connected to Him and draw us closer as we journey through life.

If you are tied to the anchor and the anchor is out there in the rock, as we are drawing closer to who we are in Christ, there is more tension. Not stress, but tension.

Don't be afraid of the tension.

Tension brings transformation.

If I go to the gym and do biceps curls with a 1-pound weight for 30 minutes, I may burn a few calories, but I will not build any muscle. Tension on the muscle is what builds new muscle. Tension is good and necessary.

Our Hope Is in Him

A while back, I was experiencing a hard time and God spoke through a one dollar cross at the corner store. When I saw it, the Lord spoke to me instantly. He said, "Your hope is in me." At the time, I was putting my hope in people being different, circumstances changing, and things becoming more comfortable for me. I was so focused on those things that I put my anchor in them. I felt unstable and hopeless because those things weren't happening. I immediately understood what He meant. When my anchor is in Him, it doesn't matter what other people are doing. It doesn't matter what my circumstances are. It doesn't matter what the reports are from the doctor. What matters is what He says.

If I believe He is who He says He is, then I believe all of those people and circumstances in my life are subject to Him. He will either change me or change things around me to bring me to the place I need to be. I'm constantly drawing closer to Him if I stay in relationship. He is my lifeline.

God wants to displace hopelessness today with hope. I want you to imagine dropping a 30-pound rock in a bucket of water. How much water will spill out? The same space cannot be occupied by the rock and the water. The water has to move out to make room for the rock. Just like that, He wants to put hope in and move hopelessness out. One of my favorite scriptures on this topic is in Romans.

May the God of hope fill you with all joy and peace as you trust in him, so that you may overflow with hope by the power of the Holy Spirit. – Romans 15:13 (NIV)

He is the God of hope. He will give you hope if you will receive it from Him. He is your hope and your anchor is secure in Him.

2

YOUR PERCEPTION IS YOUR REALITY

Your perception is your reality. That does not mean the way you perceive things is the truth. It just means the way you perceive things is the truth to you.

I went to a church service recently where I sat behind a young girl that was probably about six years old. The church service was pretty long so she kept herself occupied playing with her Barbie dolls. At one point, she stuck her Barbie doll in a Kleenex box and flew it around as if it was an airplane. Then, she sat her Barbie doll on her mom's tablet and pulled it around by the ear buds acting like it was a sled. I thought, "I would've never thought of that." While I only had a standard perception of those items, to her they were a sled and an airplane!

When I was a kid, I was very fascinated with optical illusions. I even did a science project on them. What amazes me is that, in an optical illusion, once you see it, you know it. You can't not see it anymore once it has been exposed to you!

Look at the picture on the next page. Do you see both the old woman and the young woman in this one?

Once you see the old woman, you know where to find her. It is the same with Jesus. Once you experience something about Him, it is yours. I have been healed, I KNOW He is my healer. I have been set free, I KNOW He's my deliverer. Who Jesus is to you is everything. There will be other times when we have to stand on the truth of what the WORD says is true even before we have a tangible manifestation of that specific truth in our lives. This is where the shield of faith comes in. Believe He is your healer while you are waiting for your healing. Our reality of who Jesus is, is what everything in our life centers around. Make sure your reality is based on truth!

Years ago, when I was a second grade teacher. I read a book about the solar system. I know this is common knowledge and it is something we all say all the time, but as I was reading the following sentence, it struck me in my spirit.

"Everything revolves around the sun which is constantly giving off energy."

Everything in life revolves around who Jesus – the Son – is, whether we are aware of it or not. While the truth of who He is never changes, when we have a wrong perception of who He is, things get "off." It's almost as if things start to wobble as they move around Him and we become unstable in our ways because we have a wrong perception of His character.

Is it more important to know how your King operates or is it more important to know who He is?

Knowing who He is is more important, because if you know who He is, then you will trust what He does. If you know and believe with your whole heart that He is good, and that He loves you perfectly, then you will not question His ways when they don't feel right to you. You will trust Him if you know Him. It's the same as hearing something about a good friend that seems out of character. You will automatically assume the best of him because you know him. When someone comes to you and says, "Did you hear what so-and-so did?" and it doesn't seem in line with who they are, your relationship with them assures you there must be more to the story or this report must not be true. It can be the same with Jesus when we truly know Him. In fact, there are times when we don't even need someone else's report—our own emotions and thoughts try to convince us that Jesus is not who He says He is. Having a relationship with Him will help shield against these attacks.

We are human though. It may take us a while to come to those conclusions when something hurts or disappoints us. That's OK! God can help us through those times.

When Jesus entered into Jerusalem, many people were hoping the Messiah would ride in on a warrior horse with a sword in His hand to defeat the Roman soldiers who were oppressing them. To their disappointment, He did not enter Jerusalem that way. Instead, He came unarmed, humbly riding on a donkey!

Many times, God answers prayers in a different way than we want and expect. God answered their prayers to deliver them from oppression, but He did it through His sacrifice, not a war against the Romans. He delivered them from oppression for eternity, not just the present time. His ways are higher than ours.

"For my thoughts are not your thoughts,
neither are your ways my ways,"
declares the Lord.
"As the heavens are higher than the earth,
so are my ways higher than your ways
and my thoughts than your thoughts."

– Isaiah 55:8-9

Circumstances cannot define who Jesus is. We cannot take a snapshot of our life in the moment and say, "Well, this tells me who Jesus is and I don't really like it." We are not God. We cannot always see what He is working out in our lives. His word is truth. His word is where we need to find the definition of who He is.

Knowing Jesus

We all know God is three parts. Not separate parts – three parts working in complete unity. The Trinity is something we will probably never really comprehend while in our physical bodies. While I was growing up, I knew God the Father. I don't know why, but I have always had a connection to Him and I am so thankful for that. As I came to know the power of God, it was easy to get to know the Holy Spirit and learn to hear His voice. Finding a close relationship with Jesus has been more of a struggle for me. I don't know why that is. I think it has something to do with the fact that I grew up in a church that did not emphasize Jesus as someone to have a relationship with.

It seems strange to me that Jesus was the one I felt the most distant from understanding because we actually have a picture of Jesus in the Word. I am learning to draw closer to Him.

A while back, I attended a service by Randy Clark. During the ministry time, I felt God taking away layers of hurt from the past in ways that I don't even have words to explain. I was on the floor crying out to Him and receiving His ministry. When I got up from the floor, all of a sudden, I felt connected to Jesus in a way like never before. I don't really have words to explain what happened, but I am thankful. It's possible to have a wrong perception about someone or something and not even know the details of why. I am living proof that the Lord can change your perception with truth anyway! It is so comforting to know that the Lord does not depend on our understanding to bring freedom! I am thankful to now be able to see my Savior in a better way. He knows me, and I want to know Him.

He can make you feel so special. I imagine a big grand parade going through the city streets. The King is in the parade and stops the float just to say "hello" to you. He knows your name and everything about you. He is willing to do whatever it takes to connect with you.

A Wrong Perception Made Right

One thing I had to learn about Jesus is that He cares just as much about women as He does about men. I know that sounds so elementary, but it was so ingrained in me that "a man is a leader" that, in my mind, I felt like that meant men were more important. I allowed myself to be minimized and hindered in the name of humility and honor of men. Most of these men were never intentionally trying to hurt me. I simply had a wrong perception that affected me in a negative way.

Years ago, a man named Ron invited me to his house for Bible study. Ron is one of those men I do not understand, but he is absolutely wonderful. He and his wife spend their life ministering to people wherever they are. They know no boundaries to ministry and have greatly impacted my life. These are the words he read.

When Jesus had crossed over again in the boat to the other side, a large crowd gathered around Him; and so, He stayed by the seashore. One of the synagogue officials named Jairus came up, and on seeing Him, fell at His feet and implored Him earnestly, saying, "My little daughter is at the point of death; please come and lay Your hands on her, so that she will get well and live." And He went off with him; and a large crowd was following Him and pressing in on Him.

A woman who had had a hemorrhage for twelve years, and had endured much at the hands of many physicians. She had spent all that she had and was not helped at all, but rather had grown worse— after hearing about Jesus, she came up in the crowd behind Him and touched His cloak. For she thought, "If I just touch His garments, I will get well." Immediately the flow of her blood was dried up; and she felt in her body that she was healed of her affliction. Immediately Jesus, perceiving in Himself that the power proceeding from Him had gone forth, turned around in the crowd and said, "Who touched My garments?" And His disciples said to Him, "You see the crowd pressing in on You, and You say, 'Who touched Me?'" And He looked around to see the woman who had done this. But the woman fearing and trembling, aware of what had happened to her, came and fell down before Him and told Him the whole truth. And He said to her, "Daughter, your faith has made you well; go in peace and be healed of your affliction."

While He was still speaking, they came from the house of the synagogue official, saying, "Your daughter has died; why trouble the Teacher anymore?" But Jesus, overhearing what was being spoken, said to the synagogue official, "Do not be afraid any longer, only believe." And He allowed no one to accompany Him, except Peter and James and John the brother of James. They came to the house of the synagogue official; and He saw a commotion, and people loudly weeping and wailing. And entering in, He said to them, "Why make a commotion and weep? The child has not died but is asleep." They began laughing at Him. But putting them all out, He took along the child's father and mother and His own companions. He entered the room where the child was. Taking the child by the hand, He said to her, "Talithakum!" (which translated means, "Little girl, I say to you, get up!"). Immediately the girl got up and began to walk, for she was twelve years old. And immediately they were completely astounded. And He gave them strict orders that no one should know about this, and He said that something should be given her to eat. – Mark 5:21-43

Ron pointed out that Jesus stopped for, cared for, and valued a woman. I can still hear Ron's voice saying, "Nicole, Jesus cares about women." He even called her "daughter" – the only person recorded as earning this endearment. After Jesus healed the woman who had the issue of blood, He healed a girl who was exactly 12 years old. The young girl had been alive for the same amount of time the woman had been ill. God is so amazing.

What Truth Do YOU Need?

I didn't realize how unstable I was in this belief UNTIL Jesus revealed HIS truth! Now my perception is based on actual truth and I am secure. Ask the Lord what truth He wants to bring to you. We all "wobble" in different ways. The truth makes you free.

Jesus is a warrior and He is not passive at all. He is aggressive in His love for us and passionate about the things we care about. He sees our tenderness and our dreams. He created us the way we are, and He loves us. He is patient, loving and kind. He can be all things to us that we need Him to be.

He Is

I performed this song years ago and it helped me understand that Jesus is and always has been. It reveals Jesus in EVERY book of the Bible. Look up the lyrics and let it bless you. I want to know Him in the fullness of who He is. I know that will never happen in the natural, but I want that to be my goal. I want to know the truth about Him and I want the truth to be my perception.

We need to have the victory that comes from knowing the truth about who Jesus is because who He is, is everything. We have to believe the truth about who He says He is, so we will believe Him when He tells us who we are!

"He Is" by Aaron Jeoffrey[1]

In Genesis, He's the breath of life
In Exodus, the Passover Lamb
In Leviticus, He's our High Priest
Numbers, The fire by night
Deuteronomy, He's Moses' voice
In Joshua, He is salvation's choice
Judges, law giver
In Ruth, the kinsmen-redeemer
First and second Samuel, our trusted prophet
In Kings and Chronicles, He's sovereign

Ezra, true and faithful scribe
Nehemiah, He's the rebuilder of broken walls and lives

In Esther, He's Mordecai's courage
In Job, the timeless redeemer
In Psalms, He is our morning song

In Proverbs, wisdom's cry
Ecclesiastes, the time and season
In the Song of Solomon, He is the lover's dream

He is, He is, He is! ...

"I have the right to do anything," you say—but not every-thing is beneficial. "I have the right to do anything"—but I will not be mastered by anything. –1 Corinthians 6:12 (NIV)

3

66

I am not usually a numbers girl. My husband is the numbers person in our family. He can do every kind of math imaginable and God speaks to him through numbers. The following revelation about 66 is the most powerful revelation using a number I have ever had. It has flipped my understanding in so many ways.

A few months ago, I started seeing the number 66 everywhere. I wasn't looking for it but I would glance down and the temperature would be 66 degrees, my phone battery was at 66 percent over and over again. I knew if I looked at my phone, it was going to be 66.

One day in staff meeting, Pastor Jerry was discussing what temperature to set in the sanctuary for an event. I knew he was going to say 66 degrees and he did. Later that day, I went to the Christian bookstore and they were having a sale. Guess what? It was 66 percent off. Who does that?

That was the moment I woke up and said, "Okay, God. What are you saying?" I decided to pursue His voice and began researching the number 66. It was a journey that would leave me forever changed.

The first thing I did was look in the book *Numbers That Preach*[2] by Troy Brewer. Here is what Pastor Troy wrote:

> "The number 66 is an excellent example of a witness to man or against the flesh." (p.75)

> "It is the number associated with a human being having a testimony. I think 66 has a lot to do with flesh humbling itself to the authority of God's word." (p.193)

My first inclination was to take those words and force my flesh to submit to the authority of God's Word. I decided I would eat better, be more disciplined, and exercise. It quickly turned into my own effort forcing my flesh to submit to my spirit. It didn't work. Right about the time I realized my efforts were a big bust, the words "Route 66" came to mind. I asked the Lord what He was talking about because I knew it had something to do with driving.

After I received this revelation, I received a prize at staff meeting. I have never won anything except this one time. It was the last prize drawn and it was a bag of trinkets from California. When I found this magnet in the bag, I was floored!

My friend Mason had been on the trip to California and helped choose the prizes. He walked over to me just as I was looking to see what I had won. He said he knew the gifts he chose would mean something to the person who received them. He also told me things about the number 66 that I did not realize.

Our Role

Most younger people have no idea what this is:

This is the gearshift of a manual transmission car. Let me quickly describe how to drive a stick shift. You have your gas pedal and brake. To the left of the brake is a clutch pedal.

To drive a manual transmission vehicle, you push down the clutch with your left foot every time you want to change gears. You cannot change gears unless you press the clutch. If you try to change gears without the clutch pressed down, it will grind and make a terrible noise. To drive, you press down the clutch and accelerate slowly in first gear. You let the clutch out. You accelerate until you can't go any faster, then press the clutch down again, move into second gear, and let the clutch pedal out. You do that until you are in fifth gear or to the speed you want to drive.

I remember when I first learned how to drive a stick shift. My dad let me practice in a parking lot then said, "Now drive home." I told him I didn't want to, but he insisted I could do it. As I was driving, we went up a hill. That is probably the most difficult position to be in as a new driver. On a hill, you have to balance all of those things perfectly, so you don't roll backward and hit the car behind you. I was so concerned I was going to roll backward, I popped it forward and almost ran over the missionary lady collecting money on the corner! We all survived and it's now just a funny memory. I am so happy my dad taught me how to drive a manual transmission, because the Lord spoke a powerful word to me using this analogy.

The clutch represents our role in a transition. It has to be in a position of submission for gears to shift. We are to submit and let God shift the gears and make sure we don't roll backward. We submit to Him and His perfect wisdom because He can be trusted with the power to shift the gears when necessary. He knows when we need to go faster or slower as it relates to our lives.

But How?

Let's be honest. Submitting and trusting Him with your whole heart is easier said than done when you're not sure what He's doing. The comfort comes when you realize the One you are submitting to loves you perfectly. He has a plan that is better than anything you could create on your own. Sometimes, you may question that. You think you could plan something better than God did. Maybe a relationship doesn't end or continue the way you wanted it to. Maybe you didn't get a job you wanted. Maybe there are disappointments that stir up a lack of trust. This is where the true meaning of Romans 8:28 comes into focus.

And we know that all things work together for good to those who love God, to those who are the called according to His purpose. – Romans 8:28 (NKJV)

This little verse gets quoted a lot, yet I don't think people really know what it means. The Word here says all things will work out for our good. God never promises that all things are going to be good. As I was typing this, I felt I needed to stop and listen to a video clip of Benny Hinn. Recently, he publicly rejected the "prosperity gospel" as it relates to "giving to get."

"Today, sadly, among a lot of circles, all you hear is how to build the flesh," Hinn says in the clip. "It's a feel-good message … It's all about 'feel good,' 'do good,' all that. Make money, all the rest of it. And I'm sorry to say, prosperity has gone a little crazy, and I'm correcting my own theology. And you need to all know it."[3]

Wow! This is exactly what Romans 8:28 is all about. This is exactly what 66 has meant to me. It is the flesh submitting to the Spirit, humbly, so that the Lord's purposes can be fulfilled because I trust Him. Another interesting fact – Benny Hinn is 66 years old. God really wants us to get this!

Understanding God's love for you and receiving it changes everything! The more real His love is to you, the more you begin to trust Him. The more you trust Him, the more willing you are to submit to Him. You begin to trust His ways more than yours. You begin to see His good in situations even if circumstances aren't what you prefer. You also begin to trust it will work out for good even if you haven't seen it happen yet.

Is there a place in your life where you have been resisting and the Lord is asking you to trust His love and submit? I promise the gears will shift much better if you do your part and submit to your loving Heavenly Father. The Lord spoke to me recently and said, "Submission brings rest." There are places in our lives where we have gotten so used to resisting God's perfect plan that we have actually convinced ourselves it is His will and it's supposed to be this hard. We tell ourselves God will give us the strength to get through it. In reality, we would find rest if we just submit to His plan and do the things He's asking us to do. Rest will bring restoration to those places. It's a matter of trusting the Lord with your life.

Resting in God doesn't mean that you don't do anything. It means you find the peace in the middle of the storm, activity or struggle in your life. You can find that peace because Jesus is always with you. Jenny Donnelly explained it like this in her book *Still.* "I used to think REST and stillness were synonymous with a lack of busyness. The image of the tornado gave me a new paradigm. God was saying that I could be still and experience REST right in the middle of the chaos."[4] This quote is on page 66!

True Submission

As I continued to see the number 66 on my phone and all around me, I began to understand more of what it meant for the flesh to "humbly submit itself under the authority of God's Word." My first interpretation was so wrong! The Lord showed me it really means understanding that **His Spirit is more powerful than anything in the flesh.** We know that with our mind, but if we look at our lives, there are many times we try in own effort to do what we think we should do. We try in own effort to do what we think spiritual people are supposed to do instead of using that effort to behold the One who gives us the power to humbly submit ourselves to the authority of God's Word. We use our time and energy to do the things instead of learning about the One who will do them through us.

Our own efforts may produce some fruit that lasts for a while, but it pales in comparison to the lasting fullness that can be accomplished when we allow His power to flow through us. It's about knowing Him and His power. As I was processing this with the Lord, I was watching a video on another topic. In it was the scripture Isaiah 66:1 – "Heaven is My throne and earth is my footstool." I felt the Lord when I read that. The Spirit realm is so much more powerful than what we see on the earth. His throne is a reality and it will continue forever. This earth is just temporal. My human efforts to eat better and exercise are just works of the flesh if I don't tap into His Spirit. You can do the same thing with different motives and understandings and get different results. It's not that we don't "do the things," it's how we do them that changes the outcome.

A Great Example

Peter understood that his true power came when the flesh was submitted to the Spirit. He knew that Jesus would be faithful to flow through him when he got out of the way!

A Lame Man Healed

Now Peter and John went up together to the temple at the hour of prayer, the ninth hour. And a certain man lame from his mother's womb was carried, whom they laid daily at the gate of the temple which is called Beautiful, to ask alms from those who entered the temple; who, seeing Peter and John about to go into the temple, asked for alms. And fixing his eyes on him, with John, Peter said, "Look at us." So he gave them his attention, expecting to receive something from them. Then Peter said, "Silver and gold I do not have, but what I do have I give you: In the name of Jesus Christ of Nazareth, rise up and walk." And he took him by the right hand and lifted him up, and immediately his feet and ankle bones received strength. So he, leaping up, stood and walked and entered the temple with them—walking, leaping, and praising God. And all the people saw him walking and praising God. Then they knew that it was he who sat begging alms at the Beautiful Gate of the temple; and they were filled with wonder and amazement at what had happened to him. – Acts 3:1-10 (NKJV)

Peter did not give the lame man earthly things. He gave him spiritual things. The only way Peter could give him those things is to know what he himself had. After the man was healed, he was so excited that he told everyone. He had been begging for money for so long that he was well-known. The word says the people *marveled* at this. Peter and John said:

> So, when Peter saw it, he responded to the people: "Men of Israel, why do you marvel at this? Or why look so intently at us, as though by our own power or godliness we had made this man walk?" – Acts 3:12 (NKJV)

He then proceeded to preach the Gospel, telling about Jesus' power, and many were saved. Acts 4:4 tells us about 5,000 people believed. As Peter was preaching, the religious leaders of the day were greatly disturbed because it threatened their own power. They arrested Peter and John and demanded answers to their questions.

> And when they had set them in the midst, they asked, "By what power or by what name have you done this?" Then Peter, filled with the Holy Spirit, said to them, "Rulers of the people and elders of Israel: If we this day are judged for a good deed done to a helpless man, by what means he has been made well, let it be known to you all, and to all the people of Israel, that by the name of Jesus Christ of Nazareth, whom you crucified, whom God raised from the dead, by Him this man stands here before you whole." – Acts 4:7-10 (NKJV)

The religious leaders realized they could not say anything against Peter and the others because the man was healed! They could not ignore it. They were released with a strong rebuke and ordered not to speak of Jesus. Of course, Peter declared He would not let them tell him what to do because he had to be obedient to the Lord.

*And being let go, they went to their own companions and re-
ported all that the chief priests and elders had said to them. So
when they heard that, they raised their voice to God with one
accord and said: "Lord, You are God, who made heaven and
earth and the sea, and all that is in them..."*
– Acts 4:23-24 (NKJV)

Does this remind you of another verse we read?

*Thus says the Lord:"Heaven is My throne, And earth is My foot-
stool. – Isaiah 66:1*

Prayer for Boldness

This is a prayer the people all prayed in unity. You can pray
this prayer because it applies to YOU. It will help the resurrection
power of Jesus live in you and cause your flesh to be a great witness of Him. Here's the thing. The world needs you to be a great
and powerful witness. You cannot do it in your own strength. You
need an understanding of the power you have access to through
the Lord.

*Now, Lord, look on their threats, and grant to Your servants that
with all boldness they may speak Your word, by stretching out
Your hand to heal, and that signs and wonders may be done
through the name of Your holy Servant Jesus."And when they
had prayed, the place where they were assembled together was
shaken; and they were all filled with the Holy Spirit, and they
spoke the word of God with boldness.– Acts 4:29-31 (NKJV)*

That boldness comes from knowing what you have! Let's look
back at this. Remember my first understanding of 66 was to force my
flesh to be good enough and submit to the authority of the Word of
God? Peter and the rest of the disciples give us an example to follow
in learning how to truly submit to Jesus.

The disciples walked with Jesus and were constantly presented with things that did not make sense. Still, they had to choose Jesus over and over again. Peter had to learn to submit to Him daily – like the clutch. They were with Him. They knew and felt His love. They learned to trust Him because they had a relationship with Him. Peter was not afraid to commit to the Lord because he *knew* Him. It is no surprise that when Peter talked with the man who wanted money in Acts 3:5-6, he realized that while the man was asking for an earthly thing, he had something greater to give him.

You Have Something to Give

How many times do we beat ourselves up because we think we don't have enough to give? Maybe we think we don't have enough money, time, resources, or answers for those around us. We compare what we can give to someone else and feel like we fall short. We need to know that what we do have to give is much more powerful than anything we can hold in our physical hands. Peter knew what he did have to give would change this man's mind and life forever. A domino effect of power was set in motion. They were going to pray and got interrupted by man who wanted money. They prayed for him and he was healed. People marveled at this. The Holy Spirit led them to have the opportunity to preach the Gospel. Thousands were saved. Peter and the others were arrested and able to testify to the religious leaders about Jesus once again. When they were released, they shared Jesus with the people again and prayed with such boldness it actually shook the room!

The Result of True Submission

Sometimes we read scripture and don't realize the context. Do you realize that after this prayer for boldness, they all came together in one accord? They sold what they had so that no one had need? What kind of boldness and faith in the Lord would it take for you to love your brothers and sisters so much that you're willing to give up your belongings so you can dwell together in unity?

This all happened because Peter understood what he had. That is what the flesh humbly submitting to the power of God's Word looks like. It's understanding who you are submitting to and what He is giving you. We saw what Peter's own flesh was capable of when he denied Jesus three times. Do you see the difference it makes when that flesh is humbly submitted to the Spirit and works of faith are done through Him?

When Mason explained the magnet he had chosen for the prize, he told me about the Route 66 information in *Numbers That Preach* that I had not seen because it was in a different section than I thought it would be. When I read it, I realized this story in the book of Acts is about Peter being a witness to man. The number 6 represents man and when a number is doubled it means it is a "faithful witness." You can be a powerful witness of God's power and love by truly knowing who He is and the power He has given you.

Prayer for Boldness

Let's go back to that prayer. Before we pray, I want to ask, "What are your threats?" You may not have religious leaders ready to throw you in jail like the disciples did, but we all have threats that come against us. The Lord can deal with those when we submit to Him. Is it a relationship in your life or financial struggles, health issues, or entanglements in the world? What are your threats? He has an answer for those. Romans 8:28 tells us what His plans for our threats are. Pray this prayer and fully expect the Lord to shake your world just like He did for his people in the early church. It's the same church we are in right now. The same power. Humbly submit your flesh to the power of God's word and watch what happens. This revelation changed the way I live my life. I pray it changes yours too.

> *"Now, Lord, look on [my] threats, and grant to [me] that with all boldness [I] may speak Your word, by stretching out Your hand to heal, and that signs and wonders may be done through the name of Your holy Servant Jesus."*
> *– Acts 4:29-31 (NKJV)*

4

OVERCOMING STRONGHOLDS

There are two definitions of strongholds used in the bible. One is a wonderful place of protection you can find in the Lord and the other is a wrong thinking pattern based on lies and deception. This type of stronghold is described in 1 Corinthans:

> *For though we live in the world, we do not wage war as the world does. The weapons we fight with are not the weapons of the world. On the contrary, they have divine power to demolish strongholds. We demolish arguments and every pretension that sets itself up against the knowledge of God, and we take captive every thought to make it obedient to Christ. And we will be ready to punish every act of disobedience, once your obedience is complete. – 2 Corinthians 10:3-6 (NIV)*

There are places in our minds where we have knowingly or unknowingly partnered with a lie. That lie has replaced truth for us. Rather than lining up with what God says, we live a "muted" life based on lies. We can get pretty good at it too. You can look like the most confident Christian even if you never allow truth to lead every part of your life and challenge the lies, or strongholds, you've embraced.

Let's say there's a man who looks very successful. His home is beautiful. He runs a successful business from his home; he is fit because he uses his home gym, and he also has people over to swim in his pool. His closet is filled with expensive clothes he bought online. He watches church online faithfully and loves the Lord. He is confident, happy, generous, and patient inside his home. However, the moment he thinks about leaving his home to see and experience some of the places he has seen on TV, complete terror sets in. He is afraid to fly so he will never leave the continent. He will not get on a train, boat or even drive in a car. He has a limited circle of friends because he is always at home. He is still single without children even though he wants to have a family like the ones he sees on TV. Little by little, strongholds have limited his life in massive ways.

Jesus IS Our Comfort Zone

It's easy to be the most confident Christian inside your comfort zone because your strongholds are never challenged. Your value is not determined by how far out of your comfort zone you are willing to go, how much freedom you find, or how successful your ministry is. Your value is determined by the price Jesus paid for you and He gave it ALL! There is also NO CONDEMNATION (Romans 8:1) for those in Christ who are in the process of discovering freedom. However, your victory and effectiveness in the Kingdom are very much tied to overcoming strongholds and learning to live in truth.

Lazy River or Roaring Rapids?

You may wonder if something is a stronghold or not. One simple way to tell if an area of your life is under the influence of the enemy is to ask yourself, "Am I in control of this?" Is there something that keeps coming up and you feel powerless to change it, or you feel like you have no understanding to change it? It may be a bad habit, a habitual sin, an attitude, or even a reaction to something or someone that you feel you cannot control.

A stronghold can feel like the difference between roaring rapids and a lazy river. When you're in the lazy river, you can get in and out whenever you want with ease. It's up to you entirely. When you're in the roaring rapids, it feels as if this thing is taking hold of you and you do not have complete control to stop or start whenever you'd like.

A stronghold takes root when we have an experience and the enemy comes in with a lie that "feels" true, so we grab hold of it as truth. For instance, during a hard situation, you may feel completely abandoned. Those feelings will lead you to the thought that you can never rely on anyone. At the time, it seems true. You grab hold of it as complete truth. Then, you live very distant from people because you don't want to rely on anyone. That lie has now become a stronghold that you build your life around whether you are conscious of it or not. You may know that not relying on anyone is not God's will for your life, but you find yourself acting out a different belief.

Close the Door

The enemy is a terrible houseguest! You open up one little closet in your house and say, "Okay, you can stay there." Maybe it's a "small offense" or a "little unforgiveness." But he doesn't stay there. He eventually comes out, takes over the whole room, then he's in the kitchen making dinner, and leaves his stuff in the living room. Before you know it, he is in every room of the house because you cracked the door to one little thing! The enemy has no legal ground in the life of a believer. You are hidden in Christ (Colossians 3:3) and you belong to Jesus.

> Or do you not know that your body is the temple of the Holy Spirit who is in you, whom you have from God, and you are not your own? For you were bought at a price; therefore, glorify God in your body and in your spirit, which are God's.
> – 1 Corinthians 6:19-20

You Have Authority

The enemy doesn't have authority. As believers, we have been given that.

Behold, I give you the authority to trample on serpents and scorpions, and over all the power of the enemy, and nothing shall by any means hurt you. – Luke 10:19 (NKJV)

The devil needs agreement from us to take territory in our lives. He needs us to say, "Yes, that's true" to his lies. **He is looking for access through agreement.** My neighbor does not have legal right to come into my home and steal my TV just because I leave my front door open! Access may not grant legal rights, but it does open the door to problems if the thief (John 10:10) sees a way in. There are also times when that access was granted by someone else in your life and you have to remind the devil that he needs to get out!

The weapon against strongholds is **God's truth**. God's truth exposes the lies of the enemy. When we grab hold of God's truth, it displaces the demonic so it cannot remain. We have to get rid of strongholds to get rid of a demonic presence in our lives.

If you look up the word "demon" in your Bible concordance, you will find many references. Demons are real. Jesus set people free of demonic oppression when He was here on Earth and He still sets us free today. If there were a human enemy coming to steal from you and I knew how he was going to do it, I would tell you his plans so you could protect yourself. I view demonic enemies just like that. It's important to know that a Christian will never be completely controlled by the demonic realm because we have God's Spirit and we belong to Him! However, Christians can certainly be under the influence of a demon. Deliverance is part of the Christian life you have chosen. Freedom is for you. If there a places in your life that you believe may be under demonic influence—don't freak out! We have authority over the demonic. Jesus is so passionate about leading you to freedom that He died and rose again to give you that authority. **Let's jump right into the deep end and talk about ways the enemy creates strongholds in our lives:**

Like I mentioned before, the enemy needs us to agree with him to have a demonic presence in our lives. Finding the truth will bring light to areas of your life and expose the darkness. There are many strategies he uses. Let's look at a few. If something rings true for you please continue to seek out more truth! This is just a starting point.

Sometimes, we are caught up in sin. If we ignore God's leading in an area of our lives and open the door for the enemy to come in. Remember that he is a terrible houseguest! Ask the Lord to reveal the "entry point" so you can close that door.

Other times, we have negative soul ties with people. Negative soul ties can occur when you have sexual relations with someone outside of marriage. This creates a connection between you that grants access for the demonic influences that person is carrying to also come into your life. It also entangles our souls (mind, will and emotions) in a way that the Lord never intended it to be entangled.

Soul ties do not always involve sexual relationships. They can also be formed through unhealthy relationships with a parent, friend, or a even a child. It is not that these relationships are bad, they just need to be submitted to the Lord. Often, abuse or control are part of the relationship. Seek the Lord. Is there someone in your life that seem like they are on the throne of your life instead of Jesus? Do you feel like you are obligated to make decisions that please them rather than following the Lord? Are you consumed with thoughts about them (good or bad)? This is the prayer I pray with people to break soul ties. I tell people you can gain "spiritual weight" by praying this prayer. Sometimes, you find that you are "stuck" because part of you is missing and you can't move forward. The Lord is all about restoration. He is all about WHOLENESS!

> *By the authority of Jesus I break any unhealthy soul ties between myself and _____. Jesus, I ask you to stand between_____ and myself. I send back every part of them that I have taken and I call back every part of me from _____. Jesus, I place you and you alone on the throne of my life.*

Another big area the enemy sneaks in is through un-forgiveness. Sometimes we don't even realize we have un-forgiveness toward someone. It takes courage to seek the Lord on this. He will guide us every step of the way to forgive those who have hurt us. Forgiving someone does not mean you're excusing their behavior. It means you are no longer holding a grudge against them for what they did. It means you are setting the person and yourself free! It's important to remember this. With God, you are 100% always forgiven. The word says we were once and for all made holy through the sacrifice of Jesus. Every sin we have ever committed or will ever commit is already forgiven when we are His child! You HAVE forgiveness and you can GIVE forgiveness.

> *When you were dead in your sins and in the uncircumcision of your flesh, God made you alive with Christ. He forgave us all our sins, having canceled the charge of our legal indebtedness, which stood against us and condemned us; he has taken it away, nailing it to the cross. – Colossians 2:13-14 (NIV)*

This scripture tells us that if we choose not to forgive, we will live in torment. That is exactly what un-forgiveness does. It torments! It's like drinking poison every day hoping it will make the other person sick. It doesn't work, and it only harms us. But forgiveness sets us free! (Matthew 18:21-35)

Rejection and trauma can open the door for children to receive demonic strongholds. Many of the strongholds people have to overcome are from childhood. I wish kids were off-limits to the enemy, but they are not. Many times when we seek freedom, we find the parts of our lives we struggle with are rooted in childhood trauma. God can heal these things and set us free.

Other areas Satan likes to use to immobilize us are points of weakness, such as addiction or insecurity. He also uses our spoken words against us – curses like "I wish I was never born" or "I'll never be good enough." Negative words cause agreement with the enemy.

Another area we don't think about is cursed objects. I know this sounds weird but sometimes objects can carry spirits and curses. I thought this was ridiculous, but years ago, my husband was playing a video game called The Godfather. It is a very dark video game. At the time, my son was about five years old. He was playing in his room and said that he saw a little man walk across the floor in a black trench coat. Then, I was doing dishes another day and saw something dark go by the window. We prayed about it and decided the videogame was allowing things into our home. We got rid of the video game and never had those experiences again.

Sometimes, an object leads your mind to think about something it shouldn't. Perhaps somebody gave you something years ago and it brings back bad or sinful memories. It's best to get rid of those things if you feel it is hindering your life.

The weapons we fight with are not the weapons of the world. On the contrary, they have divine power to demolish strongholds. – 2 Corinthians 10:4 (NIV)

Truth Is a Weapon

The truth helps identify strongholds. The truth will make you free. You have the Sword of the Spirit which is the Word of God. When the truth shines through, the devil will leave. The word is your primary weapon for bringing down strongholds.

> *Submit yourselves, then, to God. Resist the **devil**, and he will **flee** from you. – James 4:7*

Sometimes, we forget about submitting to the Lord. We forget to make sure our minds are in a place of receiving His truth. The truth is going to dispel the enemy in our lives.

Finding freedom from demonic oppression is a normal part of Christianity. It should be very normal for us to seek freedom in whatever way we can. Jesus died to give us that freedom. We are forgiven and made righteous by God! That is the truth.

My Freedom Story

I told you we were going to eventually dive into the deep end. I want to share one of my testimonies of defeating strongholds in my life.

Years ago, I was attending Convergence Church in Fort Worth. Stacey Campbell, a prophet from Canada, was coming to speak. I Googled her and found she was going to be at Christ for the Nations for a women's conference later that month. When I opened her website for details, I heard the Lord say, "It's time." I didn't know what it was time for, but I really felt I needed to go to the conference.

The conference was great. Many speakers I loved and appreciated were there. The first night, I cried the whole way home as I prayed through what God was doing in me. On Saturday afternoon, there was an altar call for those with a heart for missions. I went forward. As I was standing at the altar, I remembered something I had been reading in *Developing your Prophetic Gifting*[5] by Graham Cooke. He said we do not receive from the Lord in our soul, we receive from the Lord in our spirit and then our soul (mind) discerns what the Spirit tells it. I decided to try it. I said "Soul, step aside and spirit, take the lead." In that instant, I began to scream and shake. My body was doing something and my mind was wondering what the heck was going on! Jane Hamon, one of the speakers, came over and cast out the spirit of fear, the spirit of hindrance, and the spirit of shame. By the time she got to me, I was on the floor beating the floor with my fist. This all happened in front of about 300 people!

After a while, I calmed down and sat in a chair. Jane hugged me and said with a smile, "I know that was weird, but it was good. What usually takes people 12 years in counseling, God did for you in an instant. This was from something when you were a child." I just took her at her word and still had no clue what really happened. Now, I had a choice. There was a fancy luncheon during the lunch break. *Do I become embarrassed and stay away, or do I hold my head up and go anyway?* I decided to go anyway. I walked into the room and people treated me just like nothing had ever happened.

I realized deliverance and seeking freedom is supposed to be part of the normal Christian walk. We're not supposed to be afraid of it. We're actually supposed to pursue it because there is no shame in finding freedom from demonic oppression.

When I went home, I knew I felt different. I had been set free of demonic influences I didn't even realize were there. I now reacted differently when a challenging situation came up because the demonic oppression was gone. It is true that when something demonic leaves you it will try to come back. My friend Tom teaches about deliverance. He says that when something demonic is influencing you, it's part of you and you don't realize it. Once you've been set free, it's on the outside of you and you can discern its presence. It was true. It was almost as if those spirits were a cloud following me around looking for opportunities to come back in. I prayed and asked Kevin to pray with me to resist the devil and eventually it did flee. Please learn how to stay free. Fill those places with the Holy Spirit!

Let's Unpack

I have never been the same. There have been times Satan tried to come back and hinder my life. As I have grown to understand what happened at that conference, I realize that once I found freedom from strongholds in my life, I was able to truly let go and command the demonic influence to leave. The truth came in and the demons no longer had a place to hide. One stronghold that was torn down for me during the conference was about healing. I had the belief that God did not want to always heal because my brother had died. The Lord revealed truth and displaced the lie. The result was freedom!

That is the progression. First, discerning places where we have strongholds. Then, finding the truth. Next, agreeing with the truth and finally, commanding the enemy to leave. There will not always be outward demonic manifestations like I experienced. Many times, the door is shut just because you changed your mind and replaced the lie with the truth. Once you are not in agreement with the lie, the devil has no access. The door is closed, and he cannot stay. I have seen this with myself and others. The truth really does make you free. You just have to choose truth and not allow strongholds to remain.

His name is powerful and we must never forget it. We are equipped to pull down strongholds!

I do want to say that sometimes we need another person to help us walk through some of these things. Find a biblical, spirit-filled partner who can help lead you to truth. You will never regret finding freedom!

5

FREE TO RECEIVE

Kids are great receivers. I have never seen a child say, "No, thank you" to an unwrapped present sitting in front of them. The only reason a child wouldn't jump at the chance to get a present is a wound. Wounds have the ability to cause their reaction to be different than that of the excited child God created them to be. Have you ever found it difficult to receive? It's possible that is what has happened to you. Along the way, wounds have created different thought patterns and reactions that make it difficult for you to receive the good things God has for you.

Recently, I experienced a physical wound which I caused! We had just finished our family garage sale and I was exhausted and hungry. I was making myself a protein shake in the kitchen using a hand blender. I usually unplug the hand blender before I rinse it off. This time I did not. I accidentally hit the button and blended two of my fingers. I instantly held my hand up above my head and yelled "Help!" We went to the hospital, but they said they could not stitch my wound. I'll leave those details alone.

For six weeks, my fingers were bandaged. They could not get wet and I had a hard time walking without them throbbing. I was not able to wash or fix my hair, cook dinner – the list goes on. My recovery was a family effort that got me thinking about wounds.

Sometimes, wounds come because of something we did and sometimes, they come through others. In fact, we carry around wounds we don't even know we have. I have been healed of childhood wounds where I have no recollection of the event that caused them. God is not concerned with us finding out who's at fault. He wants to help you find freedom. Jesus came to set the captives free. He never brings shame or condemnation – only healing.

> *"The Spirit of the Lord is on me, because he has anointed me to proclaim good news to the poor. He has sent me to proclaim freedom for the prisoners and recovery of sight for the blind, to set the oppressed free, to proclaim the year of the Lord's favor." – Luke 4:18*

Inside Wounds

My physical wound could be seen on the outside, but emotional wounds are a different story. However, there are ways to "see" them. Wounds are sensitive and you feel them when they are poked.

Symptoms of a wound may be times when you suddenly start acting childish about something, react in anger, feel afraid, feel sick, or lash back at someone. Triggers can be a word, phrase, situation, or a certain person. I have had smells trigger wounds. Those wounds keep us in bondage. Wounds cause us to protect ourselves instead of trusting God.

You don't have the power to heal your wound on your own. It's not a matter of avoiding it in your own strength. When you do this, it is still affecting you. You do have the power to seek out the Healer and partner with Him. You cannot "will" something to be healed. It's not a matter of willpower. It's a matter of partnering with God through the process. Sometimes, the process is quick. Other times, it takes longer than you want. Either way, it is worth doing whatever God asks you to do. Embrace the process of healing and be patient with yourself.

Healing is a choice. It happens from the inside out. Wounds will limit you just like my hurt fingers did. The Lord wants to restore your freedom!

The Healing Process

As my fingers healed I was able to do more. However, they were still tender. I was still limited because I was not completely healed. My fingers looked healed on the outside, but inside they still hurt.

Many times, a wound that is healing looks ugly as it sheds the old skin and brings on the new. That's what happened to my fingers. New skin formed under the surface of the ugly old skin, but I had to let it be "ugly." I could not make the process go faster. You cannot say to yourself, "This will not look ugly and everything will remain perfectly normal while I am healing."

You have to recognize where you are and let God be with you wherever that is. We are all "in the process" in so many ways at the same time. Remember, there is no shame or condemnation for those who are in Christ. Be loving to yourself while you are healing and feeling ugly. Focus on the "new" that is emerging – sort of like that awkward phase kids go through when they lose their baby teeth. Try and recognize when others are in this process of healing. Love others though their process too! Remember, they may look perfectly normal on the outside but they aren't so great on the inside yet. They need your support. We are designed to need one another. I needed help when I couldn't use my fingers, and emotional wounds are no different. Reach out for help when you need it and don't let the enemy convince you not to!

If we don't deal with wounds, they can get infected and limit us even more. Ignoring them is never a solution. In the end, it will cost more. Our wounds also affect other people. How do you find healing from the wounds in your life?

- Be honest.
- Be okay with where you are and know you can start healing from there.
- Shut out the voice of the enemy.
- Listen and respond to God's voice.
- Know it's worth it.
- Remember that Jesus came to heal you and set you free. His mission was not only for salvation but also healing and deliverance. This is freedom.

When we are healed, we can help others heal.

Back to the topic of receiving. Receiving doesn't always come naturally. Have you ever tried to give a compliment or gift to someone who refused to receive it? It's very frustrating when you try to sow something good into someone – to speak life to them, and they refuse to accept it. It doesn't make sense. You can receive a compliment without becoming proud. You can also receive a gift when you feel like you don't deserve it. It's ok to receive! God is a rewarder whether we receive it or not!

> *But without faith it is impossible to please Him, for he who comes to God must believe that He is, and that He is a rewarder of those who diligently seek Him.– Hebrews 11:6*

Humble people can still acknowledge the good God put in them. That's the point: God gives and we get to be the receivers.

A while back, I opened my Bible and instantly heard the word "give." I looked up all of the word references to "give" in the Bible and found so many were references to God giving to us. He is a giver. Love gives. He gives spiritual gifts, salvation, His Son, blessings, provision, favor, and so much more. God also gives seed to the sower and bread to the hungry (2 Corinthians 9:10). In other words, God gives seed for us to sow into ground – people's lives – that will produce a harvest. He will lead us to know where to plant our seed. He also gives us "our" daily bread to nourish us. He gives to us so that we have what we need to be sustained and encouraged to continue. For many of us, it's easier to receive things we should give away than the things we should keep. For others the opposite is true. Both are needed and the Lord gives both seed and bread. Talk to the Lord if you struggle with either one of these. Seek help to discover if a wound may be causing the difficulty. He wants you to delight in both giving and receiving,

One of my favorite things Pastor Bill Johnson says is, "Don't sow your bread and eat your seed." You need to know the difference between what your seed is and what your bread is. How can we know the difference? We have to hear God's voice and believe what He says – even what He says about us!

"But Moses pleaded with the Lord, "O Lord, I'm not very good with words. I never have been, and I'm not now, even though you have spoken to me. I get tongue-tied, and my words get tangled."– Exodus 4:10 (NLT)

Remember the story of Moses being called by God? When it comes to the potential for success in your life, don't look at your abilities. Instead, look at what God can do through you as you become a yielded vessel. Receive what He has for you to do so you can serve others. If you don't, everyone misses out. Why?

You can't give away something you don't have. You have to learn how to receive things from the Lord so you can learn to be a giver. That is the cycle He desires to see. He knows there is joy in giving. Part of that joy is knowing what it feels like to be a receiver. I give better gifts because I have received gifts. I have learned to encourage through receiving encouragement.

I wish we were all continuously lavished in gifts and encouragement from those around us. Unfortunately, because of wounds in their lives, that is not the case. Those around us often have their own struggles that prevent them from being a "giver" of the gifts and encouragement we need from them. Please be careful not to assume that because they do not show you love in these ways that you are not loved or valued. They just aren't able to give – encouragement, kindness, time – because of their own wounds. Pray that the Lord helps them. In the meantime, the good news is you can always receive from your Heavenly Father. As you learn to receive from Him, you will find yourself filled up, healed of wounds, and empowered to be a "giver."

To illustrate this point at a recent meeting, I gave each person two oranges. I told them to pray about what God wanted them to do with them. That's exactly how gifts work. He gives to us and helps us discern how to use what He gives us. Before I could finish passing all the oranges out, I turned to find a woman had all of them sitting in her lap. She was crying tears of joy because she had come to the meeting with a great need in her life. Every person had decided they wanted to give both of their oranges to her. Wow! Sometimes we instantly know what God wants us to do with what He has given us. Other times, it takes a while to know. It's O.K. to hang onto things until we know what to do with them. Then, there are times we know that it was a God "wink" just for us and we are supposed to keep it. God's love for us is incredible. There is no way we can ever comprehend how He loves us. If we receive His love and all that it brings, there is no end to what we can give!

So if the Son sets you free, you will be free indeed.
–John 8:36 (NIV)

6

ONE VOICE

We were heading home after a family trip to Panama. It had been a wonderful time for our family to reconnect. We had planned to arrive back on Tuesday. When we were about 15 minutes from the airport, which was about an hour away from the condo we stayed in, my husband said, "Which bag are the passports in?"

I said "Oh no! Where are the passports?" Then, we remembered we had left them hidden in a drawer when someone was coming into the condo to fix something because we were not going to be there. It seemed like the responsible thing to do, but it was very irresponsible not to remember to retrieve them. We never do that! There are a lot of things we aren't very good at but forgetting passports when we are traveling internationally is not one of them.

At that point, it was too late. We had to continue to the airport. We were told we could not fly without our passports and they rescheduled us for the next flight – the middle of the night on Friday. So, we loaded the suitcases back in the rental car and booked a hotel in Panama City. Thankfully, someone helped us arrange a courier who could bring our passports to Panama City!

On the way to our new hotel, I mentioned that maybe we could see Iglesia San Jose. This was a church in Panama City I wanted to visit the entire time we were there, but I could not get my family motivated to take me. Iglesia San Jose is a Catholic church built in 1673 with an altar painted with real gold. I love old churches. While I knew it would be fun to see, somehow, I knew God also had something for me there. My son told me I must be God's favorite because He made us stay in Panama City so I could go to that church. My husband said, "God must be saying 'Kevin if you had only listened!'" I don't know if that is all true, but I do know God was at work!

The next day, we made the journey to Iglesia San Jose. It was gorgeous. I can only imagine all of the history in that one building. At one point, I sat down in the pew and began praying in the Spirit. All of a sudden, I received an incredible compassion for the Catholic people of that nation. It reminded me of two conversations with two different people on our trip. Both of them mentioned the Catholic convention was going to be held in Panama that year. This was a very big deal for the country! Thousands of people, especially young people, would be attending. I began to pray that they would have their hearts captured by the Lord and know the true meaning of what Jesus did for them. I prayed they would have Jesus in the right place in their lives. He is the way, the truth and the life. There is nothing we need to add to His plan of salvation. We don't need any other mediators because Jesus made a way for us to approach the throne of grace freely. I began to realize that every one of us can fall into the trap of carrying burdens God never intended us to carry. These burdens can be very heavy. They can also be so normal that you don't recognize them as unnecessary burdens.

At one point while writing this, I wrote down that there is an "easy solution" and I had to correct myself. Many times, the solution is *simple,* but it's not necessarily *easy* all of the time. Praise the Lord it's simple! **The solution is to only follow the *One Voice* that truly matters.**

Years ago, I was the principal of a private Christian school. In the transition between the previous administrator and myself, the school board became more active in the leadership of the school. That meant there were several of us interacting with parents and students. At one point, the chaplain said to me, "Nicole, there needs to only be one voice and that voice needs to be you." I was very okay with other people sharing the load. I did not need to be heard as the one voice all of the time. However, I completely understood what he was saying.

Have you ever tried to work for two bosses? Sometimes, I have compassion for my children because they have to live with two parents who don't exactly see eye to eye on everything. It can be confusing when you are trying to follow more than one voice. It's true that every time God led His people, one clear leader was designated. Leaders like Moses and Joshua. It is also true that we have only one Shepherd. We have only one Heavenly Father. We have only one loving Savior. We have one voice, and one voice alone, that determines who we are and what we are called to do.

I recently listened to a message by Bill Johnson. You can find it on YouTube: "Bill Johnson | Sermons 2019 | LISTEN TO GOD'S VOICE ALONE."[6] So much of this chapter was inspired by his message. The following quote changed my mind and brought me freedom in so many ways. He said:

> *"Our problem with faith is not the inability to hear His voice. It's our willingness to hear other voices."*
> *–Bill Johnson*

I like to have a tangible understanding of concepts. Imagine this: you are the soil. The Word says the seed fell on good soil. That's what we are talking about. God sends a seed to plant a purpose and a blessing in your life. You hear that truth and it is planted in your heart and begins to grow.

Now, you also hear other voices. Voices of other people, your own voice or the voice of the world around you can compete with God's voice. When those other voices are *also* planted in your heart they begin to compete for the same nutrients, sun, and space. They have the potential to choke out the good that God has planted with His seeds of truth. It's not that you did not hear God – it's that you were willing to hear the other voices.

Many times, we "know" something in our minds, but we don't "know" it in our hearts. I once had a pastor named Jeff. One thing he said that has stuck with me all these years was, "You act out your belief system." In other words, the Word has to be your truth or you will act differently. If I said I believed something, yet you see me doing the opposite, you are not likely to trust that is truly what I believe. The Lord wants us to know His voice.

The discussion about hearing the Lord and knowing what truth He wants to plant in our lives can stir up the question...

"How can I hear God?"

The Word of God is a great place to start. God will never tell us something that contradicts His Word.

Thy word is a lamp unto my feet, and a light unto my path.
– Psalms 119:105 (KJV)

In the same message I referenced before, Bill Johnson shared this insight. He said we need to focus on the fact that God's ability to be heard is greater than our perceived inability to hear. I say "perceived" because of this: you are His child. We are His sheep. The Word says in John 10 that we are His sheep and His sheep hear His voice. In the natural, if someone is hard of hearing we raise our voice, speak clearly, give eye contact, and take other measures to make sure we are understood. If we do that, don't you think the Lord is capable of making sure we get His message? God even spoke through a donkey!

Recently, I finished the book *The Search for Significance* by Robert McGee.[7] It helped change the framework of my thinking in ways I don't even have words to explain. He dug deep down into my core and established foundational truths. The basic premise is this: when we know God's truth and we truly believe what He says, we will be secure in our identity in Him. Then we are not tempted to entertain other voices.

This revelation changes everything because it destroys the lie that "I need other people's approval to be accepted." The truth will make you free! This concept may seem simple and elementary, but do not be deceived. EVERY part of our lives hinges on what we believe. Our truth HAS to come from the Lord or we will not function and experience victory from the secure identity that Jesus died to give us.

Let's Practice This...

Truth #1

Therefore, if anyone is in Christ, the new creation has come; The old has gone, the new is here! – 2 Corinthians 5:17 (NIV)

This is the truth God says about YOU! Other voices may say, "You'll never change. That's just who you are. Your past will catch up to you." If you entertain those thoughts along with the truth, eventually the truth from the Lord will be choked out by the lies of the enemy. Why? Because while you *did* hear His truth, you *also* listened to other voices, so you will not see the full benefit of that truth in your life.

Truth #2

I can do all this through him who gives me strength. – Philippians 4:13 (NIV)

Maybe God has called you to do something and you know it, but the "other" voices around you tell you otherwise. They may say, "You don't have enough time. You don't have enough money. You are crazy. That will never work."

Many times, to live for the "one voice" requires us to be a bit stubborn. I use this word in music a lot. I love to sing harmony. I tell people that in order to sing harmony you have to be a bit stubborn to stick to your part. Your mind wants to fall into the melody of the song, but in order to play your part, you need to be stubborn and focused on what you are doing. It's the same concept when you stick to the truth of what God says. The Word of God calls this being "single minded."

Your "Yes" Will Determine Your "No"

I have a friend who has struggled with drug addiction his entire life. At one point the Lord wanted me to tell him, "You need to focus on what you say 'yes' to because your 'yes' automatically says 'no' to other things in your life." Sometimes, we focus on everything we need to say "no" to and it can be overwhelming. I don't know about you, but when I feel overwhelmed I am tempted to just give up. If we hear what God has to say and say 'yes' to His voice, we will automatically say 'no' to other things that do not align with His will. It's not that people have bad intentions. There may just be scheduling issues when we don't hear the "one voice" and stay committed. If God tells me to go to a study on Monday nights and I am asked by my family to do something else, I need to first consider what I said yes to. My "yes" can automatically determine the "no's" in my life. In my friend's case saying "yes" to providing for his family would automatically say "no" to spending money on drugs. Focus on the "yes."

It needs to be said that sometimes this is not popular. Sometimes, listening to the Lord upsets other people because they don't get their way. Unfortunately, many times our greatest persecution comes from other believers. If we choose to walk in love and humility, God has provision for all of the struggles that will come from walking with Him. He is faithful. For this, Bill Johnson has another quote that makes so much sense!

> *"If you don't live by the praise of men, you won't die by their criticism."* – Bill Johnson

God's voice will lead us to life. God's voice will build us up and never tear us down. Every one of us needs to hear God's voice clearly for ourselves and for others. God always speaks life to His children. He is always leading us in love.

This concept only works if we are *very honest* with ourselves. *The Search for Significance* book exposed me to me. I needed an honest look at what I truly believed so I could understand my reactions to other people and things. When my belief system was challenged and I began to receive the truth of what God says, my reactions to other people and situations began to change.

The Word Will Help You Be Honest

For the word of God is alive and active. Sharper than any double-edged sword, it penetrates even to dividing soul and spirit, joints and marrow; it judges the thoughts and attitudes of the heart. Nothing in all creation is hidden from God's sight. Everything is uncovered and laid bare before the eyes of him to whom we must give account. – Hebrews 4:12-15 (NIV)

Let me stop here. If that's all that I ever read to you, wouldn't that sound kind of scary? I don't know that I want my sins exposed. However, the next portion of the word encourages us and tells us exactly why we can trust the Lord with everything.

Therefore, since we have a great high priest who has ascended into heaven, Jesus the Son of God, let us hold firmly to the faith we profess. For we do not have a high priest who is unable to empathize with our weaknesses, but we have one who has been tempted in every way, just as we are—yet he did not sin. Let us then approach God's throne of grace with confidence, so that we may receive mercy and find grace to help us in our time of need. – Hebrews 4:14-16 (NIV)

We can be good soil by only listening to the "one voice" and keeping our minds free from the weeds of anything that would compete with what the Lord has for us. The enemy of the great is always the good. It may be that many of the things you want to add to your life are good, but they are not in line with what God has called you to do. It may also be that you need to stand up to people who are not aligning their words about you with what the Lord says. It may be that you need to change your "self-talk" to align with what the Lord says. You are completely loved and accepted because of Jesus' sacrifice. We find victory when we come to the Lord with a repentant heart. When we keep our minds pure by the power of the Spirit, we allow the blessings of truth to prosper in our lives. Others around us need this to happen. They need us to be victorious.

My prayer on the pew at Iglesia San Jose in Panama was that knowing Jesus would bring freedom, not a burden, to the people in Panama. I pray the same for us! When we listen and align ourselves to the "One Voice," the seeds of truth bloom and prosper in our lives!

It is for freedom that Christ has set us free. Stand firm, then, and do not let yourselves be burdened again by a yoke of slavery. – Galatians 5:1

7

FOCUS BRINGS FREEDOM

There is a terrific video on YouTube about a woman who starts cleaning one thing and then gets distracted by something else. Then she moves on to that thing only to get distracted by something else. In the end, she never really gets anything done but she feels busy all day. Can anyone relate? I do. It is so easy to get caught up in "everything" that nothing really happens.

Focus actually brings freedom. Being focused and choosing what you spend your time and thoughts on can make a huge difference in your life. When you stay focused, you actually accomplish your goals. Focus brings freedom from guilt, frustration, and condemning thoughts. Another great by-product of staying focused is peace. Of course, Satan doesn't want us to have any of those things, so he is going to distract us as much as possible. Distraction is also a plan our enemy uses to keep us from our calling. All Satan has to do is distract you from the right things. He may do this with other "good things." Simple distraction can be successful in pulling you away from what you are called to do.

Planned Neglect

I love learning about leadership. One of my favorite books is *Leadership 101* by John Maxwell. It's the little book that changed my life. He shares a story about a violinist that really helped me.

"A young concert violinist was asked the secret of her success. She replied, 'planned neglect.' Then she explained, 'When I was in school, there were many things that demanded my time. When I went to my room after breakfast, I made my bed, straightened the room, dusted the floor, and did whatever else came to my attention. Then I hurried to my violin practice. I found I wasn't progressing as I thought I should, so I reversed things. Until my practice period was completed, I deliberately neglected everything else. That program of planned neglect, I believe, accounts for my success.'" – John C. Maxwell, *Developing the Leader Within You*[8]

There is something very different about intentionally choosing not to focus on something rather than allowing yourself to feel weighed down by the fact that you're not doing that "thing." It is a way of sorting things in your mind and choosing what you focus on. When you *choose* to put something aside you are being intentional and using your power to choose. This shuts the mouth of the accuser that wants to make you feel overwhelmed. One example is saying, "I am not going to focus on the laundry today even though it's piling up. This meeting with my boss is more important." Or, "I know there are dishes in the sink. However, I am going to sit down and have my quiet time with God right now." You may need to neglect "things" until the people in your life are taken care of. There will even be times when you need to choose to have fun or rest instead of accomplishing a task. Determine the priority and *plan to neglect* other things until your priority is accomplished.

Maxwell shares another powerful story about a lion tamer. Have you noticed that lion tamers always have a stool? The lion tamer holds up the stool and the lion attempts to focus on all four legs at once. Because it is impossible, the lion becomes paralyzed in a sense, and the lion tamer has complete control.

That paralyzing feeling is real. We can be so busy with so many things and not accomplish anything! Or we choose to stay on the couch in our pajamas even though we have deadlines to meet and people counting on us.

Focus especially matters in *thoughts*. It is what you choose to spend your time thinking about that creates your feelings. Those feelings ultimately lead to actions. God tells us what to focus on in Philippians 4.

> *Finally, brothers and sisters, whatever is true, whatever is noble, whatever is right, whatever is pure, whatever is lovely, whatever is admirable—if anything is excellent or praiseworthy—think about such things. – Philippians 4:8 (NIV)*

Keep Your Eyes on Jesus

We used to live in Kerrville, Texas. There is a wonderful man named Max Greiner who built a prayer garden with a 77-foot-7-inch empty cross on the top of the hill.[9] While we were living there, many negative things were happening in the world and in my personal life. I felt very overwhelmed, depressed, and hopeless about these things. It was also a time when I felt pressure to focus on things I felt very uncomfortable with. God used this empty cross to teach me something. He said, "Keep your eyes on the Me and whatever I want you to focus on will pass through the cross. Those are the things I'm giving you the grace to address in your life. Don't take your eyes off me to focus on something or someone else."

So many times, good things can demand our attention. As a mom, dad, husband, wife, friend, daughter, son, church member, or anything else we are, we can feel overwhelmed by demands. Helping people can also demand our attention. When God spoke this to me, I realized He will even cause those "good things" to pass through the cross. This will be your confirmation they are things or people you should focus on. This does not mean we are given a "get out of jail free card" from ever dealing with something difficult in our lives. It just means we can trust God's timing of when He wants us to handle it with Him. When something passes through the cross and is handled in God's timing, we also learn to see those things and people through His eyes, not our own. That is a very different perspective!

Are there things you know are passing through the cross for you right now? What is God calling you to focus on? What you say "yes" to will automatically say "no" to other things in your life. It's okay to plan to neglect the things you don't believe God is calling you to right now. Focus brings freedom!

8

GOD'S RECIPES

A while back, I felt such an urgent need to go back to the Word of God. It's time for us to know what the Word says and live it out. God gave us His Word on purpose. The Word is alive and brings life to us in every way. Jesus is the Word! That was His name in heaven before coming to earth – The Word. That's why He is the Word made flesh. When you read the Word of God, you are reading Jesus. When you seek truth, you are seeking Jesus. God's Word brings hope, healing, direction, victory, and anticipation. Sticking to God's Word is very much like sticking to a recipe.

We have all been at someone's house when they serve something so absolutely amazing, we ask if we can have the recipe. When you get home and attempt to make it yourself, you have to stick to the recipe if you expect it to taste the same. When following a recipe, we cannot leave out or exchange an ingredient without affecting the outcome.

At my house, I try to make a "healthier" version of certain recipes. I use honey instead of sugar and applesauce instead of butter. Let me tell you, it never tastes the same as a recipe made with the actual ingredients! God gives very specific recipes for certain situations in life. Do you know where the recipe for love is in the Bible?

> *Love is patient, love is kind and is not jealous; love does not brag and is not arrogant, does not act unbecomingly; it does not seek its own, is not provoked, does not take into account a wrong suffered, does not rejoice in unrighteousness, but rejoices with the truth; bears all things, believes all things, hopes all things, endures all things. –1 Corinthians 13:4-7 (NASB)*

The Consequence of Compromise

Let's say I decide not to stick to the recipe and take out patience. I will be all those things except that I'm not going to be patient anymore because people need to get with my program! I have just compromised the recipe. I cannot expect the same outcome in my relationships if I choose not to love the way God tells me to love. When I talk about the word compromise, I'm not talking about a brother and a sister deciding to share a chore rather than fight over it. In this context, compromise means knowing what is right but choosing not to do it – big or small. Bill Johnson says, "Compromise is the welcome mat to deception." It means if you continue to compromise and make decisions you know are not right, eventually compromise is going to become your normal. After a while, you will not even feel bad about those decisions. You have messed with the recipe so much that you forgot what it was actually supposed to taste like. You can correct compromise by going back to the WORD!

God also gives us a recipe for how to think...

Finally, brethren, whatever is true, whatever is honorable, whatever is right, whatever is pure, whatever is lovely, whatever is of good repute, if there is any excellence and if anything worthy of praise, dwell on these things.The things you have learned and received and heard and seen in me, practice these things, and the God of peace will be with you.
– Philippians 4:8-9

He also gives us a recipe for having unity in the body of Christ.

Unity of the Spirit

Therefore I, the prisoner of the Lord, implore you to walk in a manner worthy of the calling with which you have been called,with all humility and gentleness, with patience, showing tolerance for one another in love,being diligent to preserve the unity of the Spirit in the bond of peace. There is one body and one Spirit, just as also you were called in one hope of your calling; one Lord, one faith, one baptism, one God and Father of all who is over all and through all and in all. But to each one of us grace was given according to the measure of Christ's gift. Therefore it says,

"When He ascended on high,He led captive a host of captives, And He gave gifts to men."

(Now this expression, "He ascended," what does it mean except that He also had descended into the lower parts of the earth? He who descended is Himself also He who ascended far above all the heavens, so that He might fill all things.) And He gave some as apostles, and some as prophets, and some as evangelists, and some as pastors and teachers, for the equipping of the saints for the work of service, to the building up of the body of Christ; until we all attain to the unity of the faith, and of the knowledge of the Son of God, to a mature man, to the measure of the stature which belongs to the fullness of Christ.

As a result, we are no longer to be children, tossed here and there by waves and carried about by every wind of doctrine, by the trickery of men, by craftiness in deceitful scheming; but speaking the truth in love, we are to grow up in all aspects into Him who is the head, even Christ, from whom the whole body, being fitted and held together by what every joint supplies, according to the proper working of each individual part, causes the growth of the body for the building up of itself in love.

So this I say, and affirm together with the Lord, that you walk no longer just as the Gentiles also walk, in the futility of their mind, being darkened in their understanding, excluded from the life of God because of the ignorance that is in them, because of the hardness of their heart; and they, having become callous, have given themselves over to sensuality for the practice of every kind of impurity with greediness. But you did not learn Christ in this way, if indeed you have heard Him and have been taught in Him, just as truth is in Jesus, that, in reference to your former manner of life, you lay aside the old self, which is being corrupted in accordance with the lusts of deceit, and that you be renewed in the spirit of your mind, and put on the new self, which in the likeness of God has been created in righteousness and holiness of the truth.

Therefore, laying aside falsehood, speak truth each one of you with his neighbor, for we are members of one another. Be angry, and yet do not sin; do not let the sun go down on your anger, and do not give the devil an opportunity. He who steals must steal no longer; but rather he must labor, performing with his own hands what is good, so that he will have something to share with one who has need. Let no unwholesome word proceed from your mouth, but only such a word as is good for edification according to the need of the moment, so that it will give grace to those who hear. Do not grieve the Holy Spirit of God, by whom you were sealed for the day of redemption. Let all bitterness and wrath and anger and clamor and slander be put away from you, along with all malice. Be kind to one another, tender-hearted, forgiving each other, just as God in Christ also has forgiven you. – Ephesians 4:1-32

I have read this passage so many times. During times of discord in church, or just in relationships, this passage has grounded me and brought clarity. If we stick to this recipe for unity in the body, guess what we're going to get? Unity. It's a recipe!

The ingredients have already been provided.

God tells us what ingredients we need and how to use them. At my house, my daughter is the "ingredient getter." I get the recipe out and I tell her to get all of the ingredients and put them on the table. She goes to the refrigerator or the pantry and gets everything she needs. Who put those ingredients in the pantry or in the refrigerator? I did. I not only gave her the recipe, I provided the ingredients. It is her role to access them. She has access to every ingredient she will need. God is the same way with us. If God has given us a recipe to follow, He will be faithful to give us the ingredients we need to find success. We always have access to the fruit of the Spirit. We just have to be mindful of them and allow the Spirit of God to work in our lives. When we do that, we have consistent access to those ingredients as we create the recipe He's called us to.

Sometimes, there is not a specific recipe and you are able to decide what ingredients you want to change or leave out without ruining the dish. Maybe you want to make pumpkin bread instead of zucchini bread. Maybe you don't want to use basil and you choose to use oregano instead. It may alter the outcome, but it still tastes great! It's your original creation!

It's no secret that I am not a cook. I cook for my family to survive! Every once-in-a-while though, I try to make something good. One day, Jade wanted meatballs. I looked up recipes for sweet-and-sour meatballs and decided I would just take my knowledge of what ingredients might work and create something on my own. An absolute miracle occurred – it worked! They were good. God gives us freedom in so many areas. Sometimes you are able to choose your own ingredients and how they are put together.

There are times we know a recipe by heart. (I don't have many of those, but you probably do.) You don't even need to measure the ingredients. You just know what to do. Like times when we have the Word in our hearts and we automatically live our lives out of that truth. Then, there are recipes we don't know as well and we have to keep referring back to them. A new recipe may require us to not take our eyes off of it. It's not yet familiar to us. Learning new things from God's Word can be like this.

Whatever recipe God has called you to create is an invitation from Him. It's an invitation to partner with Him in a relationship, ministry, business, or new way of thinking. As we create things in partnership with God. It's also important to remember He is a Master Chef. When we have a recipe that doesn't go as planned, He is able to add things to create something beautiful. The Word says He "works all things for the good of those who love him and are called according to His purposes," right? He's a great redeemer.

So, don't worry about those recipes that haven't gone very well. Just step back to the Word and let Him send you for the ingredients!

9

WHO YOU ARE IN CHRIST

In the Bible, there is a special chest called the Ark of the Covenant. It was made of wood covered in gold and it contained items that represented God's covenant and power. These items were Aaron's budding staff, the 10 commandments, and a pot of manna.

The Ark of the Covenant brought favor. Wherever it was, that city prospered in every way. It was quite a process, but King David finally brought the Ark of the Covenant to his city. When it arrived, he was so excited to have the Ark of the Covenant that he took off his kingly robe that set him apart from all the common people and simply became a worshiper as he danced for joy in the streets. Without his robe, he looked like everyone else. His wife Michal saw him uncovered and dancing in the streets and the Word says she, "despised him in her heart." David's response to her was that he would do EVEN more undignified things for the Lord than that! God must have taken her attitude pretty seriously as well. The scriptures say that she was barren her entire life because of that. I believe it's a warning to us that despising things of the Lord can produce barrenness in places of our lives. Her attitude certainly didn't stop King David from celebrating and allowing the Lord to prosper him.

I Have a Robe.

In this world, I am not a king or queen. However, I am a wife, a mom, a church member, teacher, sister, minister, business owner, a singer, a daughter, and many other things. The many titles and responsibilities I carry around can become pretty heavy and stressful. They feel like I'm spinning plates like they do at the circus! It can seem as if those roles are *who* I am, and those titles define me. It's easy to get caught up in *what we do* as our identity. We tend to put people in categories according to what they *do*, not *who* they are.

The account of King David dancing in the streets reminds us of who we truly are. At the core of our being, we are created to worship the Lord as a child of God. He is our Heavenly Father.

There is neither Jew nor Greek, there is neither slave nor free, there is neither male nor female; for you are all one in Christ Jesus.– Galatians 3:28

This truth levels the playing field in so many ways. It creates an attitude of humility as we understand we are no better or worse than anyone else. God loves us as His children and we can rejoice in Him. That is who we truly are. It also reminds us God loves us as His child no matter what! We all have different robes, but He loves us because we are His child. His love and our identity in Him will never change because it is based on who *He* says we are – not on anything we do!

Your Soundtrack

God is continually speaking words of life over us and He wants us to listen. He wants us to hear those words and believe them with our whole heart. If we don't believe what He says, we are telling God we don't believe *Him*! The Bible is very clear about who we are in Christ. God's words are where we need to find our identity. He needs to be the one to tell us who we are. Not our thoughts. Not our feelings. Not our experiences. Not other people, but the Lord God Almighty Himself!

His words should be the continual soundtrack in our minds as we approach life and everything in it. It can be difficult to receive these words of truth when everything in your life is screaming otherwise. Don't let the enemy convince you God is a liar. *Think about what you are thinking about!!* Are you thinking and speaking positive things about yourself? Ask yourself, "Would God tell me that?" If He wouldn't say it to you, STOP saying it.

Be honest and hear the words of discipline the Lord may be speaking as well. He is a loving Father. His correction in our lives is *for* us — not Him! His correction is to bring freedom to our lives. Old wounds may be preventing you from receiving His voice in that way. You can trust Him with *you*. He is the perfect parent!

And have you completely forgotten this word of encouragement that addresses you as a father addresses his son? It says,

"My son, do not make light of the Lord's discipline, and do not lose heart when he rebukes you, because the Lord disciplines the one he loves, and he chastens everyone he accepts as his son."

Endure hardship as discipline; God is treating you as his children. For what children are not disciplined by their father? If you are not disciplined—and everyone undergoes discipline—then you are not legitimate, not true sons and daughters at all. Moreover, we have all had human fathers who disciplined us and we respected them for it. How much more should we submit to the Father of spirits and live! They disciplined us for a little while as they thought best; but God disciplines us for our good, in order that we may share in his holiness. No discipline seems pleasant at the time, but painful. Later on, however, it produces a harvest of righteousness and peace for those who have been trained by it. – Hebrews 12:5-11 (NIV)

When the Lord disciplines us it is ALWAYS to call us *up* into who we are in Christ. His discipline never shames, condemns or belittles us. It's crucial that we know this truth. King David knew this. King David knew that His relationship with the Lord was secure no matter what title he held or what how many mistakes he made. You can rest in that too. It's the same God that loves YOU!

It is important to speak words of life over yourself and own them as yours. Jesus died and rose again so these words would be true! Remember, God loves you. Not just 'all of us' but He loves **YOU!!** Believe who He says you are! Rejoice as a worshiper of the Lord just like King David. Trust the core of who you are as a child of God to lead you and equip you in all the "other robes" you may wear.

10

NEW WINE SKINS

Neither do people pour new wine into old wineskins. If they do, the skins will burst; the wine will run out and the wineskins will be ruined. No, they pour new wine into new wineskins, and both are preserved. – Matthew 9:17 (NIV)

There was a time I could not get away from thinking about new wineskins. It consumed my thoughts. In Bible times they didn't have barrels and bottles to store wine in. They used actual animal skins that were prepared to hold the wine. I researched what that parable meant. This is what I learned: New wine is in the process of fermenting. That means gases are being released and, in that state, it's sort of effervescent. The old wineskin is rigid and brittle. It cannot handle the constant movement and change of the new wine. If you put new wine inside an old wineskin, it will burst. It cannot contain it, and the new wine is lost. However, a new wineskin is flexible and can handle the movement, the life, of the new wine. Of course, we know Jesus is not just talking about wine. He is talking about our mindset. In this passage, He was telling the religious leaders of the day that the new way of life He was bringing would not fit in the old mindset. It was the new covenant that could not be contained by the old.

As I studied about wineskins, I was determined to not be an old one! I wanted to be the one who could handle the new things Jesus had for me. So, I was on a mission to change my mindset about everything. I began working at changing old habits that were holding me back. I challenged my ways, changed my schedule and anything else I could think of.

New Wine Skins = New Wine

One day, I was unloading groceries and realized, "That means I'm going to get new wine." As I am writing this, I realize that "random moment" had more meaning than I thought. A vehicle symbolically represents ministry. When I got my van, I knew it meant my ministry in the Kingdom was growing from a car, or family-sized ministry, to a van. What was I doing when I received this revelation? Putting groceries *in* the van. I was receiving what I needed. Wow God!

Why would I work so hard and not keep my eye on the reward? Why was I so focused on becoming the new wineskin that I completely disregarded the whole purpose – to *receive* new wine? The Lord is a rewarder.

And without faith it is impossible to please God, because anyone who comes to him must believe that he exists and that he rewards those who earnestly seek him. – Hebrews 11:6 (NIV)

Not long after that, I was driving down the road and God spoke to me. He said, "You have to know that you are worthy of receiving new wine." Is that what was stopping me? He meant I could work really hard to become a new wineskin but not receive the wine because I didn't believe I was worthy. I thought I was trying to be humble, but this challenged me. Was I disqualifying myself and that's why I subconsciously didn't even think about receiving the reward? Self-worth makes all the difference in the world. Apparently, it's important to God that we know we are worthy. He wants us to get our self worth from the true source. Your value comes from Jesus. In this revelation, knowing you are worthy because Jesus made you worthy *is* the new wineskin you need to receive the new wine!

Value

I love thrift shopping. I like to find a value – a hidden treasure. When Kevin and I were first married, I would come home, lay everything out on the bed, and show him what I got. I was proud of my finds. I didn't put my toilet paper or my dish soap on the bed, rather I laid out the things I was proud of and excited about. The other day, God reminded me of that and told me that's exactly how Jesus presents us to the Heavenly Father. He is so excited about you!

However, a willingness to pay a high price determines value. Unlike my thrift deals, sometimes I am willing to pay full price because I know it's worth it. That's why real gold, great guns, and expensive cars are so exciting to purchase. In that same way, Jesus determined your value of on the cross. He paid the ultimate price for you and He is the only one who determines your value. Not anything or anyone else. Not your actions, your feelings and, praise the Lord, not your thoughts!

Your identity, who you really are, is created by who you are in Christ. You are priceless. There is no end to what He will do for you. He knew you before you were formed in your mother's womb, has always loved you, and always will no matter what.

If you don't believe and receive your value from Him, you live as if you're in poverty when, in reality, you are wealthy beyond measure. When you receive Him and believe Him, you can live as the bride of Christ –not like a beggar. It's not because of what *you did*. It's because of what *He* did. It takes a new wineskin to receive the new wine. The "new wine" is knowing you are valuable, loved, needed, and worth fighting for.

Jesus gave us something to remember how valuable we are to Him.

And he took bread, gave thanks and broke it, and gave it to them, saying, "This is my body given for you; do this in remembrance of me." In the same way, after the supper he took the cup, saying, "This cup is the new covenant in my blood, which is poured out for you." – Luke 22:19-20 (NIV)

The New Covenant is different from the old. The New Covenant offers wholeness and eternal life though accepting Jesus. You can take communion for many reasons. He says, "Do this in remembrance of Me." It's not remembrance like someone you may have known who has passed away. It's remembrance of what He did and remembering you have a King who is alive, well, and functioning in your life at this very moment. The Lord also wants you to remember just how much He values you. He wants you to remember He paid it all for you. That's your value! Receiving His love, the new wine, will change your life.

11

BE TRANSFORMED

My brother used to have Transformer toys when he was young. These are toys that look like a car, truck, or some other vehicle, but they can be transformed into robots. As Christians, we are called to be Transformers too.

(A Living Sacrifice)

Therefore, I urge you, brothers and sisters, in view of God's mercy, to offer your bodies as a living sacrifice, holy and pleasing to God—this is your true and proper worship. Do not conform to the pattern of this world but be transformed by the renewing of your mind. Then you will be able to test and approve what God's will is—his good, pleasing and perfect will.
– Romans 12:1-2

The Transformer toys could never fight the battle before them without transforming into a robot. A car can't fight an enemy, but an armed robot can. They fulfilled their purpose by transforming.

That's what we believers do! Our minds are transformed as we become more like Jesus. The armor of God is a major key in your transformation because it's the mind's job to guard the heart.

Finally, my brethren, be strong in the Lord and in the power of His might. Put on the whole armor of God, that you may be able to stand against the wiles of the devil. For we do not wrestle against flesh and blood, but against principalities, against powers, against the rulers of the darkness of this age, against spiritual hosts of wickedness in the heavenly places. Therefore take up the whole armor of God, that you may be able to withstand in the evil day, and having done all, to stand. Stand therefore, having girded your waist with truth, having put on the breastplate of righteousness, and having shod your feet with the preparation of the gospel of peace; above all, taking the shield of faith with which you will be able to quench all the fiery darts of the wicked one. And take the helmet of salvation, and the sword of the Spirit, which is the word of God; praying always with all prayer and supplication in the Spirit, being watchful to this end with all perseverance and supplication for all the saints... – Ephesians 6:10-18

Here is why your mind needs to be protected. Your thoughts create your feelings and your feelings direct your actions. It starts in the mind!

THOUGHTS ->FEELING ->ACTIONS

I don't put my shoes on and just automatically have peace or put my belt on and know truth. The armor of God is for the mind, not your body. Your enemy attacks your mind. With the full armor of God, you can have victory and freedom in your thinking.

As a Christian, your spirit is secure, but your mind can have strongholds. Many times, the stronghold comes from something in your childhood or was not your fault. You are still called to find freedom from those strongholds. It's your responsibility. I know that doesn't sound fair, but that's how it works. The Lord helps us take back what the devil has stolen.

There are also places in your mind that you actually open up to your enemy through choices you make. You may not be aware of these strongholds, but they will eventually be exposed. Darkness can only exist in places where you close God out. Think about that. Darkness, not difficulty, can only exist where the Light (Jesus) is not!

Compromise Can Open the Door

One of my favorite Bill Johnson quotes is, "Compromise is the welcome mat to deception."

Let's talk about compromise. It sneaks in and eventually becomes your normal. When you throw a shirt on your bedroom floor and you don't pick it up, it soon becomes a "few" shirts, and eventually, it becomes a pile of clothes in the corner. Before you know it, you can't even see the floor. Having clothes on the floor became your "normal." It happened one compromise at a time.

I love workout video quotes. This is one of my favorites:[10]

> *"Transformation is not a future event. It is a current activity." – Jillian Michaels*

This means my choices today are building my experiences for tomorrow. I cannot count the times I have wanted to make a withdrawal from something I never deposited. I can't expect my kids to behave in public if I don't train them at home. I can't expect to run a marathon when I didn't do the daily routes to train. Just like that, transformation can be positive or negative. Your choices decide. You either transform one way or the other.

Have the Right Appetite

You and I need to be hungry for the right things. Have you ever been to an event where they had incredible food, but you ate before you came because you didn't know they would have a meal? You don't have room for the good stuff! Don't be full of what the world has to offer. It only satisfies temporarily, but it's enough to make you miss what God has for you. It's not that God can't redeem things. He can and will. There is no condemnation for those in Christ, and you can start walking in the right direction from where you are right now. He will help you! He's not mad at you. You are in Christ!

The joy of the Lord is our strength. Knowing the presence of the Lord is our strength. Make room for Him in your heart and in your life. Let Him live in EVERY part of your heart. Making the choice to *know* Him in everything will give you strength to do what you're called to do.

> *"When you fix your thoughts on God, God fixes your thoughts."* – Buddy Owens

Be transformed and find victory on the battlefield of your mind!

12

THE WHOLE STORY

Some things just go together. You don't think about one without the other. Things like salt and pepper, cookies and milk, Bert and Ernie, needle and thread, peanut butter and jelly. Sometimes you need one to make the other work just like shampoo and conditioner, water and coffee beans, bow and arrows.

In the same way, there are truths that go together. They don't function if you separate them. There are many scriptures that do not work if you leave part out. You need to know the "whole truth" to find the victory you are looking for. Let's look at some truths in the Bible that are sometimes told in part.

And we know that in all things God works for the good...
– Romans 8:28 (NIV)

We have all heard this scripture quoted many times. It's a wonderful promise, but there is a qualifier to receive this promise. Do you know the other part?

"...of those who love him, who have been called according to his purpose."

If you don't love Him, there is no guarantee everything will work out for good in your life.

Have nothing to do with the fruitless deeds of darkness, but rather expose them. – Ephesians 5:11

This one can get some people very excited about going around telling everyone what they are doing wrong. Finally, we have permission to point out the flaws! If you only read this one scripture you might think that is exactly what God wants you to do. However, there is some jelly to this peanut butter.

Instead, speaking the truth in love, we will grow to become in every respect the mature body of him who is the head, that is, Christ. – Ephesians 4:15

Wait! You mean I have to love them to speak truth? This is the powerful other part. To point out the darkness, I have to love these people. When I follow the whole truth, I expose the darkness in their lives *because* I love them. I'm not trying to be critical. I also know I need to follow the Holy Spirit's leading in if, how, and when to approach them. I must seek the Lord and get my heart in alignment with how He sees the person before I expose their darkness. When I do this, I am in alignment with the heart of God and the outcome will be very different than just running to a person and exposing their sins.

There are also some truths from the Bible that don't work without the other verses to complete them. You can be working really hard to believe and apply part of a truth from the Word and not see the fruit you expected. You may be missing the other part that creates the Whole Truth!

This is my favorite passage of scripture:

Rejoice in the Lord always. I will say it again: Rejoice! Let your gentleness be evident to all. The Lord is near. Do not be anxious about anything, but in every situation, by prayer and petition, with thanksgiving, present your requests to God. And the peace of God, which transcends all understanding, will guard your hearts and your minds in Christ Jesus. – Philippians 4:4-7 (NIV)

I can be begging God for peace but if I am bound up with worry, there is no way I can rest in His peace. I am making a choice to stay anxious. I need to look at the other part – "my part" – of His recipe for peace. I am supposed to rejoice in Him, be gentle, cast my cares on Him, thank Him in advance for taking care of what is troubling me – then, His peace will guard my heart and my mind.

Submit yourselves, then, to God. Resist the devil, and he will flee from you. – James 4:7

Sometimes, we recite "resist the Devil and he will flee" without acknowledging the most important part of this truth: "SUBMIT to God." How many times have you felt like the devil just kept coming at you over and over again? You were doing your best to resist, but it just kept happening? Maybe the "submission" part of this truth is what you were missing. There may be part of your life where you are not submitted to God and you are out of alignment with His truth. If you submit to the Lord and come into alignment with His ways, you will find the freedom you are seeking from the enemy's attacks. You actually have authority because you are walking in His will. This is all done through *His* power and *your* choices!

The Right Perspective

Things make more sense if you know the whole story. Now let's apply this to the "one anothers" in your life. If you are a parent, you know exactly what I am talking about. Actually, this applies to most adults. When there is an argument between your kids, if one kid tells you their side of the story, you know you don't have the whole story. When the other kid tells their side of the story, you can usually piece together what actually happened. Sometimes, even with both kids telling their "side," you still don't have the whole truth! They may not be trying to withhold information. They only have their perspective to share. Still, you need the whole truth! If you don't know the whole story, you may assume certain things about people. Social media makes this all too easy. It allows you to see snapshots of people's lives that you may be tempted to judge. Maybe you see someone you know has gone on vacation and you know they didn't have the money. You think they're being irresponsible, but if you knew the whole story, your perspective would be different. Maybe another family gifted them their time share for the week and paid for their gas because they knew they had not had a family vacation for years. You never know. Only God knows the whole story. He knows the circumstances, back story, heart, and mindset of those involved. It's a perfect perspective.

> *Jesus replied, "You do not realize now what I am doing, but later you will understand." – John 13:7(NIV)*

He is the only one who has all the pieces to the puzzle of our lives. He understands the beautiful picture He is creating from your life and the lives of those around you. We only get one piece at a time. That one piece may make absolutely no sense! But when that random piece begins to fit perfectly with another, and then another, we begin to trust His ways. There have been so many jobs, relationships, and choices in my life that did not make sense. They didn't line up with my plan. They were pieces that didn't seem to fit. As time went on, they began to make sense. That random job actually prepared me for something bigger. The relationships were exactly the connections

I needed. After a while, I started to trust that the seemingly random pieces in my life would fit perfectly into His plan. All that matters is hearing His voice!

The Lord knows the whole story – the good, the bad, and the ugly – and He still loves us perfectly. It's also true that we should give grace to ourselves and to one another even though we may not know the whole story. He has shown us His heart and He will help us love like He does. We don't have to *know* the whole story. We just need to trust the One who does! It would be impossible to know every word of scripture but it IS POSSIBLE to know the author.

Jesus **IS** Truth.

Jesus said to him, "I am the way, the truth, and the life. No one comes to the Father except through Me." – John 14:6 (NKJV)

Receive all of Him. Open your heart to receive and live the whole truth of His Word. Ask for eyes to see people and yourself the way He does. Look for the jelly when all you have is peanut butter. He will lead you into all truth because He is so faithful!

I can do all this through him who gives me strength.
– Philippians 4:13

13

THE LORD DIRECTS OUR STEPS

I woke up on a Sunday morning with the words "The Lord directs his steps" on my mind. I decided to do a word study in my New Spirit-Filled Life Bible, which I highly recommend. I feel that too many times, Bible commentaries become legalistic and religious when the actual Word of God is not that way at all! This commentary is actually Spirit Filled!

I looked up many scriptures about God directing our steps. Later, we went to church and the pastor was talking about walking in the newness of life.

> *Therefore, we have been buried with Him through baptism into death, so that as Christ was raised from the dead through the glory of the Father, so we too might <u>walk</u> in newness of life.*
> *– Romans 6:4 (NASB)*

He talked about the walk we have and the steps we take toward new life. **Walking in new life requires** *steps* –intentional steps that are directed by the Lord.

A man's heart plans his way, But the Lord directs his steps.
–Proverbs 16:9 (NKJV)

How many times have we experienced that? We have everything planned out and if all things are executed perfectly, everything will be just right. Then we find out God has a different plan! At that point, we have a decision to make. We can choose to be stubborn and stick to our ways or be humble and follow the Lord's leading. I can't tell you how many times I have planned gatherings at my home, lessons to teach, or even conversations in my mind and had them completely redirected by the Lord. However, I cannot think of a time when He redirected me that it didn't work out better than I planned. That doesn't mean everything I thought would happen happened. My objectives may never come to pass, but the Kingdom objectives the Lord had planned were accomplished by the power of His leading. Planning is a great thing. It provides momentum so the Lord can steer us. Don't stop planning! Just be willing to take a different route if the Lord has a different way.

Unknowingly Led

My Pastor Leanna gave a great illustration of a time when she unknowingly brought a group of women into a restaurant she would never have chosen on her own. She didn't realize that this particular restaurant was designed to have an atmosphere of being rude and crude on purpose! Leanna was tempted to leave but remembered that the Lord directs our steps even into places we may not normally go. She and the women stayed in an uncomfortable situation and God redeemed it beautifully by bringing their waiter back to

Jesus before they left! It is a great story of how sometimes our loving Father is directing our steps and we don't even realize it.

This brings me to free will. It is a choice to let the Lord direct your steps. 1 Corinthians 13:5 says love does not control because "it does not seek its own way." That means that at any moment, we are free to take the steps He leads us to – or not. If the Lord forced us to follow Him, our actions wouldn't be a chosen response. God is love, therefore we always have freedom to choose.

That being said, just like in Leanna's story, sometimes God is directing your steps and you don't even realize it. Most of us know this scripture:

Trust in the LORD with all your heart,
And lean not on your own understanding;
In all your ways acknowledge Him,
And He shall direct your paths.

– Proverbs 3:5-6 (NKJV)

The Spirit-Filled Life Commentary digs a little deeper into these verses. Check it out:

Intimacy and Spiritual Breakthrough: FAITH'S WARFARE. Two words in this passage are especially significant – the words "ways" and "acknowledge."

The word, "ways" (Hebrew *derek*) means "a road, a course, or a mode of action." It suggests specific opportunities a person may encounter on a recurring basis. The most common "segment of opportunity" we experience regularly is each new day. It is as if this passage suggests that in all our "days" we should acknowledge God, and in so doing, He will direct our paths.

Of equal significance is the word "acknowledge" (Hebrew *yada'*). Elsewhere yada' is translated "know," meaning to know by observation, investigation, reflection, or firsthand experience.

But the highest level of yada' is in "direct, intimate contact." This refers to life-giving intimacy as in marriage. Applied to a spiritual context, it suggests an intimacy with God in prayer that conceives and births blessings and victories. Joined to our text in Proverbs, we might conclude that if in all our "days" we maintain yada' (direct, intimate contact with God), God *promises to direct our paths toward fruitful, life-begetting endeavors. (Jeremiah 33:3/Acts 6:1-4)*[11]

This commentary tells us that if in all our "days" we "know" Him, He is going to direct our steps. He will guide us through relationship.

To me, the word "acknowledge" brings forth the connotation that you "consult" with someone. I could say "God, this is what I want to do. What do you think?" Then I get His opinion and make my decision. However, this verse in Proverbs tells us something completely different. We are to abide in Him at all times rather than consult with Him before just doing our own thing. Abiding in Him is a much better way to live.

King David understood this walk with the Lord. He knew that many times, what God led him to do didn't make sense to him. He passed this wisdom to his son, Solomon:

A man's steps are of the LORD; How then can a man understand his own way? - Proverbs 20:24 (NKJV)

That is good news! It means we don't have to understand "the way," we just have to know Him and know He is leading us. How many times have we ended up in situations or relationships where we wonder, "What in the world happened!? How did I get here?" Then, we realize God has given us influence in that situation. Maybe you ended up in a job you were not qualified for; maybe you didn't even ask for it, and God used you to bring great change. Or, you felt like you needed to go to Walmart even though you didn't need anything and you ended up praying for someone in crisis.

Even in Small Things

Sometimes the steps He leads you to take don't seem so "life changing" but we can be encouraged to know He is still directing our steps. I was packing for a women's cruise once and felt like I needed to take a black Sharpie marker. Why?? I packed it and while we were on the cruise one of the women in our group stood up and said, "Does anyone have a Sharpie marker so we can sign this t-shirt?" I said, "I do!" On our last trip to Panama I felt like I needed to take butterfly stitches. So I did. The last night in our condo Kevin was cutting vegetables and deeply cut his finger. I had stitches. Otherwise, we would have spent our last night trying to find a hospital in a foreign country and someone who spoke English! Those little things have encouraged me to listen to the whisper and follow through on things that may not make sense. There have been lots of times when I followed through and nothing significant happened but I am willing to take the chance now!

Sometimes, the steps you *don't take* are more important than the ones you do. For example, if there is an argument happening that I am tempted to engage in. It doesn't matter if I do the laundry, make a cake, or go outside. What matters is that I *do not* choose to engage in a fruitless argument.

Many times, the steps God leads us to take are not ones we like. Remember the scriptures about leaning not on your own understanding? Those words are true. When we know Him, we know God is good – that He is a good Father and where He leads us, He's going to provide every bit of what we need. Because of this, we can trust His guidance.

Sometimes, we get stressed out worrying about what steps we should take. "What should I do? What should I do? What should I do?" After studying the Word, it becomes apparent it is less about knowing what steps to take and more about knowing our Heavenly Father and staying close to Him. Did you notice the Proverbs 3 scripture says, "In all your ways *acknowledge* Him and He will direct your steps." Knowing Him is the key.

We are human. Sometimes we're going to miss steps along the way. God is such a great redeemer and He is so loving in His ways. We need not worry or stress out over times when we step in the wrong direction because He will help us get back on track. Remember, it's not about the steps. It's about knowing Him.

Knowing Him will lead you in the right direction. He always leads us to life!

14

WHEN GOD SAYS "GO"

Note to the reader: This story contains times when Kevin and I heard the Lord clearly and took steps of faith. Not all events in our lives look this way. ☺

You may hear this one story and think, "Oh, my goodness! They're just willing to follow the Lord radically in everything!" While we do try to follow the Lord in everything, there are parts of our lives where we are still working on obedience. It's also true that not everything the Lord asks you to do requires such big steps. Taking huge steps for the Lord without first hearing Him can create problems of their own!

I also want to say this is *my* story. Kevin has other parts of this story he tells that are just as amazing. This is *my* perspective, and these are the shared things we experienced. He's actually writing a book called *Why Can't I Hear God?* So, you can get his book when it comes out and hear his side of the story.

Therefore, as it is written: "Let the one who boasts boast in the Lord." – 1 Corinthians 1:31 (NIV)

We have to remember that. Any time you hear a testimony of God's goodness in somebody else's life, the enemy will try to steal, kill, and destroy any of the good parts you can receive. He will come in with jealousy. He will come in with doubt and unbelief. We just bind that right now in Jesus' name. I pray that you would hear my words and know I am boasting only in the Lord. He is not a respecter of persons. He will see your life and meet you where *you* are to advance *you* in the way that He needs to.

Story Time! Sometime in the year 2007, my husband, Kevin, started seeing 10:16 on the clock all the time. At the time, we were going to OpenDoor Church and Pastor Troy taught about God speaking through numbers. We began to understand that God is speaking in so many different ways and if you pay attention, you'll hear Him more clearly. We both started seeing 10:16. One day, Kevin said, "Nicole, I think this is about where we're going to live." There was a County Road 1016 near our house. We often drove up and down that road asking, "Lord, is there a house here that we can live in?" But nothing settled. Nothing came to pass, so we just kind of tucked it away in our hearts.

Tuck It Away for Later

I want to stop right here, there's a Scripture in Luke where it talks about how Mary tucked things away in her heart. When the angels appeared to the shepherds, they declared awesome things about the newborn Messiah. The shepherds came to see Jesus and they shared what they had been told with Mary. This is her response:

> *But Mary kept all these things and pondered them in her heart.*
> *– Luke 2:19*

She didn't reject them. She didn't fear them. She didn't question them even though she didn't understand. She treasured and pondered it in her heart; she held on to it. A while later, Jesus is missing for three days and she can't find her son anywhere! She finds Him hanging out with the teachers in the temple and He says, "Why are you worried about Me, don't you know that I have to be about My Father's business?" Then, the Scripture says, "But His mother treasured all these things in her heart" (Luke 2:51 NIV).

Those are just two times when Mary had to just treasure things in her heart that she didn't understand. Don't you know that happened all the time? Probably every day of Jesus' life things happened that made her say, "What?! That's not normal." Because she didn't understand, all she could do was hang on to those things. She did not let doubt and unbelief steal it. She treasured or valued it in her heart and it brought peace.

> *"In order to have a peace that surpasses all understanding, you have to give up your right to understand."*
> *– Bill Johnson*

If I'm fighting to get my mind around something so it makes sense – if I want to know the details and what's going on – I can get so bitter, angry, and stressed out that there's no way peace can lead me because I'm resisting it. Colossians 3:15 says "let" the peace of God rule in your hearts. "Let" means it's a choice. When peace comes, it's because you're giving up your right to understand. You have peace. Jesus gave it to you. It is a fruit of the Spirit. You just have to make sure you keep it! God is creating your destiny, let go of your need to understand, to be in control, to have things fall into your timeline and let Him create that destiny. Don't get stressed about it because that can make it take longer. Sometimes, I think we can delay and even miss and hinder things because we're not allowing God to create in us. Rest in His peace and have childlike faith that He is God and you can trust Him. That's what Mary did.

111

Where and When

So, back to 10:16. We drove down County Road 1016 and we didn't see anything there. Nothing came of that for nine months. We were just hanging on to that partial revelation. Then, we went to a prophetic conference in a town called Weslaco. We packed up the kids and drove down to South Texas. On the way back we stayed at a cabin on the Frio River. It was so beautiful, and we came through Kerrville on our way home. We stopped and ate at Cracker Barrel for breakfast and I said, "This feels like home." I am definitely the feeler of the family! On the way back home, Kevin said, "Pull out a Texas map and see if there's a highway 10 and a highway 16, and where they intersect." I pulled up the map – this was before GPS – and it was Kerrville! That was a Holy Spirit moment. The black dot was right there on Kerrville. There was no denying it was the Lord. We had driven past it, but now we knew there was a big sign that said, "Kerrville" right at the intersection of highways 10 and 16. 10:16 was no longer a mystery.

Now we knew *where* we were supposed to go, but we didn't know *when* or *how*.

We vacationed in Kerrville a few times after that and loved the area. Still, we didn't have an understanding of what God wanted us to do. I was telling Kevin the other day that we were so patient back then! We just held on to it.

Kevin's parents are from Canada and they had come to visit in the fall of 2009. When I dropped them off at the airport, I picked up the phone and said, "Kevin, let's go somewhere before Jade turns two and we have to buy her a plane ticket." Her birthday was in less than two weeks. We were just crazy and had a lot more money back then. That was a Tuesday and we were in Cancun by Thursday. It was 3 in the afternoon; we walked into our hotel room and the clock said 10:16. When we left the room, Kevin glanced at the clock as he closed the door. It was 10:16. He said, "It's time. It's time to go." And I said, "Okay, let's do it."

We came home and got the house ready to put on the market. We thought selling the house would be our trigger. That made sense. We were willing to go whenever, we just thought God wanted us to sell the house first. Then, I had a dream.

In my dream, Kevin and I were on an airplane and the plane didn't have enough fuel. It couldn't get high enough so we had to switch planes. After we switched planes, I said, "Kevin, I'm so nervous we're not going to be there in time." He pulled out a day planner and said, "Don't worry. We'll be there by 3:52."

Kevin is the numbers person in our family but I had a numbers dream. After praying about what it meant, I finally decided to look up the 352nd day of the year – December 18. I said, "Kevin, I think we're supposed to move on December 18." He agreed. So, we made plans to leave on that day even though the house had not sold. We didn't even realize until later that December 18 was the day after Andrew would be finished with school. God is pretty good at timing things!

Now, we knew *when*!

Making Plans

Then we really started thinking ahead. We needed a place to live in Kerrville, so we planned to look for a house the day after Thanksgiving. The week *before* Thanksgiving, Kevin took Andrew camping.

I was working in the church nursery the Sunday he was gone, and I just had this feeling. So, I called Kevin from the nursery on his way back from camping and I said, "I think God wants us to go look for a house this weekend, not next weekend." I cannot say how much I appreciate Kevin's support, because if I really think God is leading me to do something, he's willing to take a chance.

Kevin and Andrew got home, unpacked, and had showers! Then we booked a room at Days Inn, re-packed the car and drove to Kerrville. We started looking for a house to rent. We didn't want to buy a house because we had no idea what the communities were like or what area of town we wanted to be in. We didn't have much luck. Kerrville was not that big and there weren't many homes to rent, especially not the ones we were looking for. Kevin needed an office at home so we decided to call homes that were for sale to see if they'd be interested in renting. I remember sitting at the hotel watching him on the phone when one realtor said, "No, that owner won't do it, but I do have this other house. I think he may be willing to list it for rent. It's been on the market for a while. I can show it to you tomorrow."

Because we were so intrigued, we decided to check out the house the night before. On the way, we drove by Impact Church. We saw on the sign that Bill Johnson was there, so we just stopped in and listened to Bill Johnson preach! By the time we went to the house, it was dark, so the next day, we went to see it. It was 4,200 square feet, plenty of rooms, cabana with a hot tub, 1 bedroom cabin, laundry chute from the master bedroom to the laundry room. The master bedroom had a sitting area and a gas fireplace in it. Jade's room was huge. Each kid had their own bathroom. It had a lighted tennis court, a working antique phone booth, a beautiful backyard view of the city and was on five acres!

It that wasn't enough, back at the hotel when I was praying, I felt like God said, "There will be flowers in the kitchen." Do you see the flowers in the tile above the stove? It was confirmation.

The monthly rent was right at the top of our budget. It was a miracle. It was a confirmation that we were where we were supposed to be because He had prepared a place for us. We signed the lease. Had we not gone that weekend, the house probably would not have been available. God knows the timing!

In faith that everything was going to work out, we had already decided not to enroll Andrew for the spring in his Fort Worth private school. The administrator of his school thought we were a little crazy. We were giving up his place in the class before we knew what was happening! I started researching schools in Kerrville. We found one we really liked and went to introduce ourselves to the board president. We were just waiting for everything to fall into place before we made a decision. Between Thanksgiving and Christmas break, the school called and said the last second grade spot was about to fill. We made another trip to Kerrville, signed the lease papers, and interviewed to get Andrew into school, then drove back to Fort Worth the same day.

It's Not Always Easy

On the way to Kerrville, Andrew was crying because he adored his teacher in Fort Worth. He was seven and we were about to put him in a brand new place. He was going to love that place, but he didn't know that yet. It was the first time as a mom I really had to make a big life choice that my kids weren't really excited about. It weighed on my heart so much. It made me understand a bit more of the Lord's perspective. It helped me understand the times He tells us "no." He wants us to trust Him even when it's hard, even when we have to let go of things we love. Sometimes, following God means you're going to let go of things you don't feel like letting go of because there's nothing wrong with them! It also taught me that even when you are following God, other people may not be comfortable with your decisions. Follow Him anyway! God will work it out.

On December 18, we packed up the house and drove. We knew no one in Kerrville. We had no connections there, no job there – we were just going because God said go. When we arrived, I had so much fun exploring our five acres with my city kids. I also realized I had gotten so busy while living in Fort Worth that I was missing out on Jade. She was two and when they're small it's easy to just cart them around everywhere. They don't really have a voice to say that you're not actually spending time with them. They just kind of go along. When we got there I was like, "Wait! Who are you?" I didn't realize I had gotten so disconnected from her. I feel like God pulled me into another place just in time – before being disconnected became our normal. I'd love to say that I learned my lesson and don't ever get busy and disconnect with my family. It's easy to do that sometimes but I do know better now. When the Lord reminds me not to go down that road again, I know what He's talking about.

Come Away with Me

When everything settled from the exciting move to Kerrville, we rested. It felt very, very strange. It was the strangest spiritual time I've ever had in my life. I remember lying in bed telling Kevin that he was going to have to give me extra grace because there was something going on with me. I did not understand it or know what it was, just that it was God. What was happening was no one knew me there. I had no titles, no credentials. I had no one to say, "you're so good at this!" God stripped me of all that stuff. I didn't feel like I had any purpose.

If I had to pick one place I learned my true identity in the Lord, it was Kerrville. It began a time where I just had to say, "Okay Lord, what do You say?" Sometimes, God will lead you in those ways and places because He wants that one moment with you. He wants you to get to that place where you say, "God, I don't care what anybody else says. What do You say?" I call them the "come away with me" times and that was a big one! It's possible to have a "come away with me" time in the middle of a crowd or while you are in the process of your everyday routine. God knew me so well. He knew I'd probably still listen to other people and that's why He took me out of the busyness. It was going to be a very challenging time and I understood that.

I spent the next few months connecting with the three, lovely people in my circle of influence. We played outside. I watched cartoons with Jade and we participated in school and church. I spent time with God on my back porch swing watching the deer walk through the yard. It was actually a very sweet time.

New Opportunities

After Andrew's first semester, I was asked to be on the board of his private school. There were some challenges with the administrator and shortly after being on the school board, I was asked to be the administrator. The board president, and I were standing in her back yard and she asked me if I'd ever thought of being a private school administrator. I said, "No, and I don't want to." God kept revealing He was opening that door for me. Eventually, I accepted the position.

I was invested in the school and already helping quite a bit. I was already seeing things I could do that that would be of value to the school.

It was hard at first. It required so much cleaning up and putting structures in place. I was there 60-plus hours a week and couldn't have done it without Kevin. If Kevin had not been working from home with flexibility, there's no way that I could have done what I was supposed to do at that time. But I loved it. Eventually I didn't have to be at the school every day so that I could be at home. I even had a little table, toys, and a nap mat in my office at the school so Jade could come to work with me if I needed her to. The Lord knows what you need and He is the creator. He will make a way for you to walk in what He calls you to.

The Lord Equips the Called

I was amazed I could go from stay-at-home-mom to running a school. All of a sudden, I found myself in charge of budgets, dealing with parents and students, picking out uniforms, ordering marketing materials, and writing curriculum. I was like, "They're letting me do this?" I realized I had been trained for this position though other events in my life. I didn't know I was in training, but God's plan is perfect. King David was prepared to slay giants. He faced a bear and a lion before he faced Goliath. That's when I understood this truth: God does not call the equipped. He equips the called.

He is faithful to prepare you. Along the way, He also granted me wisdom that I knew was straight from Him because, in the natural, I had no prior knowledge to draw from. I boast only in the Lord. He is so faithful! I needed to go through the process of learning to seek Him, and Him alone, for my identity and security before He could place me in that position at school.

I called Kerrville the "Fisher Price Little People Village" because it only had one Wal-Mart, one post office – one of a lot of things! I remember telling my mom this community was so different because you *always* see someone you know. I called it accountability because I treated my kids a lot better in Wal-Mart because somebody I knew was probably watching! In fact, Kerrville was so small, I was looking at a table I really wanted on a Facebook buy-sell-and trade group. Later that day, I was at the grocery store and I saw it driving past on somebody's car. I said, "Well, I guess it sold." But in that simplicity, there was a lot more peace. We met some great people. The kids got to explore along the river, go fishing, kayaking, hunting, and camping – all things not readily available in the big city. It was a different kind of life. The deer would just walk down the streets in the middle of town. We also moved four times in Kerrville, but every time, I got rid of more stuff. For me, there was s spiritual connection to that. I was being set free and learned how to let go of things I didn't need for the next season.

Full Circle

After four and a half years in Kerrville, we felt it was time to move back to the Fort Worth area. I had heard God tell me we would move back, I just didn't know when. Then, God allowed the school, jobs, relationships, and church to sort of become dry, so we would know this season was coming to an end. When things that used to be life-giving become dry, it's important to know it may not be that anything is wrong. It may just be a sign that it is time to be planted in a new field. I know my spiritual journey of identity, a time of reconnecting as a family, and being a principal at the school were all part of the purpose God led us to.

Shortly after we decided to move back, I had another dream about living in an apartment and the whole cycle began again! That story is for another time. I will say this though, Kerrville was training for the next season. We moved back to the metroplex area on 10/16/14. God is so good!

Lessons Learned from the Kerrville Adventure:

I think in following God we have to remember that there is no "final destination." You have free will and choice. You can be completely 100% saved and choose not to follow God in the adventure He has for you. I know it's true. But if you want to be a radical Jesus-follower, you need to know that you will never be able to say, "I have arrived! I don't have to do anything, ever again. I have achieved the ultimate ministry! I am here, and everything is done for me!" It's never going to be like that. Do you know why? The Kingdom is *progressive*. We could have been offended that God didn't want us to stay in Kerrville, but thankfully we weren't.

One thing moving to Kerrville did for me is I no longer have forever-plans. I know that sounds depressing, but it's exciting to me. Before we moved, I think I had in my mind exactly how my life was going to be – my husband, my kids, my ministry, my house and what cars I would drive. I had everything planned out. Now, I don't have it all planned out. If God says "move tomorrow" that's what I will do because I trust that whatever is on the other side is better. It's better that I listen to Him and follow Him. So, I don't have forever-plans anymore and I don't feel unstable about that. I know my future rests in the Lord.

God will use things that mean nothing to everyone else to show you the something that He wants *you* to see. You know why others don't get it? Because your God is talking to *you* about what *you* need to know. Trust His voice.

One other thing I know about following God is you need to be courageous enough to believe Him. Do you know why the Israelites did not enter into the rest? Unbelief. Unbelief is what keeps you from resting.

To follow God, you have to actually *follow* God. Did you notice we had to actually do some things? We did actually go somewhere. We did have to wrestle with emotions. We did have to let Him into our hearts. We did have to actually move. We had to pack a house and everybody knows how fun that is. We had to move four times! When you follow God, it's not works. It's faith. It's living your life out of that faith and through His grace because He gives you His empowering presence to do these things. It's not works. If you get it backward, you'll know right away because there'll be a lot of grumbling and complaining. But if you do it through His grace, it changes everything.

To most people, 10:16 on the clock would seem like a really stupid thing to base your life on, but it changed our lives. Kerrville in itself did not change my life. The city did not change my life. God used Kerrville to change me.

What Adventure Does God Have for You?

What has God spoken to you? Be courageous enough to believe Him. Remember what He spoke to you and be courageous enough to believe Him. There's a book called *The Dream Giver,*[12] by Bruce Wilkinson. It is a mind-changing book. Sometimes, if you understand the process, you value it more. This book will do that for you.

The adventure He has for you is the process to produce the fruit He has planted in you. Most times, we don't know right away what God has called us to do. Just keep following Him even though you may have no clue where He is leading you. Eventually, there will be a moment where you look at your life and see what He has known all along. He's always known who you are and what you were made for. He put that gift in you. Many times, the *adventure* is the key that starts the process that allows your soul to experience what your Spirit already knows.

God has that for all of us. God will speak to you in ways that mean something to *you*. They may mean nothing to me, but they mean something to you. You have a choice. You can trust Him and walk forward or not. It's hard to hear from God if you don't trust Him. If I don't trust the Lord, I'm not even listening because I don't care what He has to say. Even if He told me the absolute truth, I probably wouldn't believe it.

Now, it's true that God can intervene. He talked to Saul before he became Paul. As believers, we can deny being able to rest in Him because of unbelief. Unbelief is linked to not trusting. If I trust He's going to lead me step by step every single step of the way – that He loves me and has the best intentions for me – I'm trusting and believing at the same time. It goes together and there's incredible rest and grace in that!

I wanted to tell this story to stir up what's in you. What adventure awaits? You don't even have to leave your house to have an adventure with Him. Seek, ask, find and go!

15

DEALING WITH DISAPPOINTMENT

When dealing with disappointment, the first truth you need to know is:

God does not *give you* sickness, poverty, or oppression of any kind to *help* you learn something.

That is a lie from the devil. It is important to understand the difference between Him *allowing* things into your life from being the source of it.

God **IS** love.

Love is patient, love is kind. It does not envy, it does not boast, it is not proud. It does not dishonor others, it is not self-seeking, it is not easily angered, it keeps no record of wrongs. Love does not delight in evil but rejoices with the truth. It always protects, always trusts, always hopes, always perseveres. Love never fails. – 1 Corinthians 13:4-8 (NIV)

Jesus tells us what He came to do for you and me.

"The Spirit of the Lord is on me, because he has anointed me to proclaim good news to the poor. He has sent me to proclaim freedom for the prisoners and recovery of sight for the blind to set the oppressed free, to proclaim the year of the Lord's favor." – Luke 4:18-19 (NIV)

You need to know and embrace the truth that Jesus is in your life to bring victory. Although He can certainly use hard trials for good, He is not the source of them.

I experienced one of the hardest trials of my life when I was 19 years old. My brother Eric, who was 17, died suddenly of bacterial meningitis. He got sick and within 24 hours, he died. I was away at college and did not make it in time to see him. I had spoken to my mom on a Sunday morning. She said Eric was at a friend's house and wasn't feeling well so they were bringing him home. She never called me back. I tried and tried to call her and my grandmother, but no one answered. Finally, I got a hold of a neighbor and she said "Nicole, it's not good." This was before cell phones and no one was home to answer.

I called the hospital and made plans to fly out. It was the strangest feeling to pack knowing I may need something to wear to my brother's funeral. Wow, that just hit me as I was writing it. When I finally arrived at the airport in Lubbock, I was so sad to see my mom and stepdad waiting for me. I knew it meant he had died because she would not have left him. I held her and screamed in the middle of the airport. I couldn't help it. It was a sad ride back to the house. I could share many more details about that week, but I just wanted to share the beginning of that story.

God was so faithful to carry us through that time. Friends and family were so helpful. A couple of weeks after the funeral, I returned to college. About a week later, I was talking to my mom on the phone and there was something that didn't sound right in her voice. I kept asking her if things were OK but she wouldn't tell me what was going on. Finally, I said "Mom, please tell me." She just didn't want to put more hurt on me. My mom is incredible.

When Eric died, my mom was pregnant. It was a big deal and we were all excited about my new baby brother. After the funeral, she had a sonogram. During that routine appointment, they found that my unborn brother, Tanner, had died. His death had nothing to do with meningitis or stress on my mom. It was a rare circumstance that could not have been prevented.

When she told me this, it was the only time in my life I have truly been angry with God. I got off the phone and went straight to the prayer closet. I got on my knees and I said, "God, what the hell are you doing? That's too much!" I talked to God about my anger, hurt, frustrations, fears, and disappointments. I didn't pull away from Him – I ran to Him. At first, my motivation was to tell Him how wrong He was. After a while in His presence, my heart – not my circumstances – changed.

In that long conversation with God, I reached the conclusion I had nowhere else to turn but Him. I realized He was my only source of hope. I ultimately said, "I don't understand Lord, but I trust you." That was the first time I ever prayed those words. I have prayed them a lot since then!

God is never offended at our hurt even when our emotions manifest as anger toward Him. He knows our heart. We are His children. He knows us better than we know ourselves. If we take *all of us* to Him and choose to walk in relationship with Him through the good, the bad and the ugly, we will always see the power of His redemption in our lives.

Of course, I would like to have my brothers back. It was a long journey to heal from those losses and God has been faithful to carry me through. He has also been faithful to bring good into my life through all circumstances.

And we know that in all things God works for the good of those who love him, who have been called according to his purpose."
– Romans 8:28 (NIV)

Don't Get Stuck

I have learned to trust Him even when I don't understand His ways. I have learned to value each day. I have chosen to live by the idea that "If you have something good to say you should say it." Not only because tomorrow is not promised, but because it would be tragic if someone lived their whole life and you never shared something positive and encouraging for or about them.

I also grew closer to the Lord. When I was young, it was easy to ride on the coattails of my family when it came to my faith. When Eric died, that changed for me. I realized God's promises had better be real because I need to know where my brother is. I would love to have my brothers back, but I am grateful for what I learned through the process of grieving their loss.

God did not kill my brothers or inflict the pain that came with their deaths. In His sovereignty, He allowed it for whatever Kingdom purposes. I have to trust in that or I will become bitter, resentful, calloused, angry, and judgmental toward God.

I believe we need an "I don't know category" in this life. This is where we file the hurts, disappointments, and confusion that doesn't fit anywhere else in our mind's filing system. Our minds are built to reason. We cannot help but want to file something in the good or bad categories. Sometimes, things don't neatly fit in a category and it paralyzes us. We cannot move forward until we learn to give it to God and move on in the truth of *who* God says He is. That's when we receive peace.

Most of the time we want to know "why" something happens. While that seems like a fair question to ask, it rarely leads to peace. God's "why" and our "human reasoning" don't always agree. It is much like a five-year-old asking a parent why they have to do something. You can tell them exactly why and they think your answers aren't good enough. Then, they feel even more agitated that they have to do it! His thoughts and ways are not ours. This is where making the choice to say, "I don't understand Lord, but I trust you" can help us move on and not get stuck in anger, bitterness, fear and resentment.

Years ago, my husband and I were hanging out in our swimming pool and He said, "Many times, our minds are like water. When it is all stirred up and stressed out, it is cloudy and hard to see. But when it is settled, it is clear, and we are able to see." I was impressed. I even shared that awesome revelation with friends. A few days later, he told me he heard it in the movie Kung Fu Panda.[13] It was still great truth though.

The Lord added something else to this revelation. Often, life can appear pure and settled, but as soon as an event, thought, or emotion stirs things up, *everything* that has been left unresolved comes to the surface. Unresolved hurt and disappointment get stirred up every time a problem or stress arises. In that moment, you are not "just" dealing with the situation at hand. You are dealing with *all* the unresolved issues *and* the one at hand! That can feel overwhelming but Jesus says, "Blessed are the pure in heart for they will see the Lord."

A Pure Heart

If I want to see what God is doing, I need to keep my heart pure because it effects how I see, experience, and react to future events. In reality, I can't keep my heart pure on my own. It is not a job I do on my own apart from God. I have to 'choose' to let God in, then He can help me with those places. Having a pure heart means trusting Him with the disappointments in my life. The sooner we choose to trust Him, the more pure our glass will be! This has nothing to do with your righteousness (right standing). You are washed by the blood of the Lamb and made perfect by what Jesus did. Having a pure heart is connected to your victory and freedom in life.

It's also important to deal with disappointment before it opens the door to a critical spirit. This happened to me just recently. I found myself complaining so much that even I was annoyed at me! When I stopped to ask God what was going on with me, He revealed several areas of disappointment that had turned into unresolved hurt which opened the door to a critical spirit. It's not wrong to be disappointed. (Someone needs to hear this.) It's not wrong to have needs. Denying you are disappointed can trap you. Pretending something doesn't hurt for the sake of others doesn't help anyone. There are times when you only process your disappointment with the Lord and that's OK. You should use wisdom in who you reach out to, not everyone needs to know everything, but reach out if you need to. Invite the Light to come and heal you!

Now, I have also had lots of experiences where I failed to trust God. In one particular experience I also failed to hang on to the belief that He allowed something and would use it for good.

My 14-year-old son, Andrew, has a drone. He spent his Christmas money to buy it. He had such a great time learning to fly it. He even purchased accessories to make it more fun. We were walking home from the park and he was flying it at the very edge of the parking lot before we turned the corner to the sidewalk. I thought he was just trying to annoy his sister with the noise (a common occurrence). I didn't tell him to stop because I was in the middle of a conversation with my father-in-law. The drone landed in the road right in front of us. I froze because I couldn't believe he did that. He seemed to take forever to go get it and as he finally moved toward the drone, a car ran over it. We all stood there and heard the "crunch" as the drone was crushed.

Andrew grabbed the drone in disbelief. A loving and compassionate response would have been to tell Andrew I was sorry and helped him assess the damage. I am sad to say that wasn't my response. I said, "What the heck, Andrew?" Then, I proceeded to tell him everything he *should* have done to avoid this. He responded with such maturity. He said "Mom, I didn't mean to do those things you are saying on purpose and now you are yelling at me before I can even look at the drone." He was right. I realized what was happening. This incident had pushed another button of disappointment in me I didn't realize was there – disappointment *for* other people.

I knew how much he cared about his drone. He didn't have the money to buy a new one and neither did I. Sometimes, disappointment shows up as anger. I apologized to Andrew and explained this to him. He forgave me, and I learned there are other places of disappointment hiding in my heart that I need to deal with.

We aren't weak or crazy for feeling disappointed. Many people in the Bible experienced disappointment. Joseph, Mary and Martha, Abraham and Sarah, King Saul losing the Kingdom to David. The disciples were disappointed after Jesus died. The thing about these accounts of disappointment is we get the privilege of reading the beginning, middle, and the end of the story. We know Joseph eventually found out it really was God's son Mary was carrying. Lazarus rose from the dead, Isaac was finally born, David was an awesome king.

Our story is still *being* written so some things will remain in the "I don't know category." Because we know *who* God is, we know He has an eternal purpose for whatever He allows.

Sometimes, the hurt of disappointment gets carried around and becomes heavy. Know this: God never intended for it to be that way. Jesus said:

> *"Come to me, all you who are weary and burdened, and I will give you rest." – Matthew 11:28 (NIV)*

Ask the Holy Spirit to reveal what disappointments you may be carrying. You may be surprised at what comes up. You may find that you have experienced the same struggles over and over again. God is inviting you to overcome that disappointment with Him and break the cycle. Unresolved childhood disappointment can certainly carry into adulthood. For example, if you really wanted a bike for your birthday when you turned seven and you didn't get it, you may have a hard time getting your hopes up for good things to come to you.

Remember that you don't need to dig up every disappointment you have ever experienced. Trust the Holy Spirit to lead you through this process. Write down your disappointments. Give them to God, then have a fire or shred them to remember that moment when you chose not to hold onto them anymore. When a thought comes back about something you let go of, deal with it through the Holy Spirit. You may still remember details but by giving the disappointment to God, the emotions will not control you and prevent you from moving forward. Many times, it is helpful to say, "Thank you, Lord, that I can trust you with this and know you are taking care of it." God will give you hope instead of disappointment. God is our hope. He is our everything!

> *May the God of hope fill you with all joy and peace as you trust in him, so that you may overflow with hope by the power of the Holy Spirit. – Romans 15:13 (NIV)*

Be patient with YOU! Dealing with disappointment can look a lot like the grief process or a physical healing. It is a healing of the heart. The Lord can heal you in a moment, walk you through a journey, heal you of everything at once or one hurt at a time. It doesn't matter how – what matters is He WILL! He is your healer. You can trust Him with every tender place in your heart. He loves you perfectly!

And we know that in all things God works for the good of those who love him, who have been called according to his purpose.
– Romans 8:28 (NIV)

This is a promise we can all hold onto and apply to our lives. I have heard it said God will never take something away unless He is going to give you something better. Praise the Lord for the times we get an upgrade after disappointment. Not every circumstance ends this way though. My brother died and I don't believe God "took" him from me. I certainly didn't get a better Eric in exchange. (Although I did get a new little brother and sister later on!) This is not what this passage means.

There will be times when things happen, and you absolutely hate the circumstances. Working all things for your good means that *if* you love the Lord you will see good brought through hard circumstances. The good will be worked for His purposes. This is where confusion can come in.

Here's another *if*. I am careful not to place burdens on people, but here is the truth: our submission to the Lord determines our outcome. You will see good if you are looking for it. When disappointment comes, you have the freedom to stay angry and bitter for as long as you like. Or you can seek the Lord in those places and see the good. Time doesn't heal: God does.

My husband's friend was telling him about a new drone he bought. In the spirit of swapping stories, Kevin shared with him what happened to Andrew. The man told him to bring Andrew over and he would give him one of his! Andrew ended up getting a drone exactly the same as the one that was run over and another drone that was even better! God has a plan for everything He allows! While this is a story of material upgrade, He always has an upgrade available to us in our walk with Him. Look for it!

Now all glory to God, who is able, through his mighty power at work within us, to accomplish infinitely more than we might ask or think. – Ephesians 3:20

We have a Savior that understands what we are facing in this life. He understands disappointment. I believe He felt disappointment when Peter sunk after the first few steps on the water, unbelief hindered miracles, the rich young ruler chose his possessions over following Him, the disciples fell asleep in the garden and many other times. Some people may say that Jesus could never have been disappointed because He already knew what would happen. I believe He still felt disappointed because His heart still wanted a different outcome.

Jesus still loved, hoped, and went to the cross for us. We are children of God living under the promise of the New Covenant, He is not disappointed in You! God does not remember your past sins, you never earned His love in the first place and God knows the end of your story! I pray that this truth brings you freedom and encouragement to take your disappointment to Jesus and find wholeness.

16

BEING

Recently, I read the story of Jacob, Leah and Rachel for the first time in a while. Later, I went to church and was talking to a friend about something regarding pets. All of a sudden, she said she used to have goldfish that got spots all over them and she found out it was fish lice! While I was talking to her, her son had a toy horse with spots on the back and the entire time he was saying, "Look spots, look spots."

I thought that was strange. The next morning, I was reading Jeremiah and one of the verses talked about a speckled bird. I was like, "Okay Lord, what's going on? Do you have something more for me to see in the story of Jacob regarding the speckled, spotted, and colored flock?" When the Holy Spirit keeps throwing something in front of you, it's a good idea to pay attention.

I looked back over the story, which is in the book of Genesis. Jacob was Esau's brother and Isaac's son. He was the younger of the two brothers and was called the "supplanter" because he grabbed the heel of his brother Esau when he was being born as if he was trying to overtake him. Later in life, his mother, Rebecca, convinced Jacob to steal Esau's birthright. After Esau found out, Jacob fled in fear for his life.

While he was hiding, he met Rachel and fell in love. He worked seven years for her father, to earn the right for Rachel to be his wife. Her father, Laban, swapped his other daughter, Leah, into the ceremony to be married to him first! Jacob was angry and disappointed. Even though Laban relented and allowed him to marry Rachel a week later, after that he worked another seven years in order to have Rachel. Through this, they all lived with Laban and Jacob watched over Laban's flock.

Laban was greatly blessed because God was blessing Jacob. After a while, Jacob felt it was time for him to earn his own wages and go his own direction. The Bible does not state clearly if the Lord told Jacob to say this, but I have a feeling he was led to do it. He told Laban he would only take the speckled, spotted, and black sheep of the flock as his own. This way, he would take the lesser and less common of the flock. He would always be able to say he had been honest because the outward appearance of the flock would prove it. Laban agreed; they separated the flock and Jacob continued to watch over Laban's animals.

Here is what Jacob did following the separation of flocks:

"Agreed," said Laban. "Let it be as you have said." That same day he removed all the male goats that were streaked or spotted, and all the speckled or spotted female goats (all that had white on them) and all the dark-colored lambs, and he placed them in the care of his sons. Then he put a three-day journey between himself and Jacob, while Jacob continued to tend the rest of Laban's flocks. Jacob, however, took fresh-cut branches from poplar, almond, and plane trees and made white stripes on them by peeling the bark and exposing the white inner wood of the branches. Then he placed the peeled branches in all the watering troughs, so that they would be directly in front of the flocks when they came to drink. When the flocks were in heat and came to drink, they mated in front of the branches. And they bore young that were streaked or speckled or spotted. Jacob set apart the young of the flock by themselves, but made the rest face the

streaked and dark-colored animals that belonged to Laban. Thus, he made separate flocks for himself and did not put them with Laban's animals. Whenever the stronger females were in heat, Jacob would place the branches in the troughs in front of the animals, so they would mate near the branches, but if the animals were weak, he would not place them there. So, the weak animals went to Laban and the strong ones to Jacob. In this way the man grew exceedingly prosperous and came to own large flocks, and female and male servants, and camels and donkeys. – Genesis 30:34-43

The Word never says if Jacob had not done those things, he would not have been blessed with more flock. If you remember, even Laban said, "The Lord has blessed me on your account." Later in chapter 31, God tells Jacob He has done this for him. So, the question is, did Jacob need to be busy doing those things to be blessed?

Was this his own self-effort or was he led by faith to do these crazy things God was going to bless? The truth is we don't even need to know. It doesn't matter. God blessed Jacob – period. God didn't rebuke Jacob for doing it nor did He give us any record that He told Jacob to do these things. He just blessed Him!

What I kept thinking about is this:

How do you know when God wants you to do something or when He just wants you to be still and trust Him to work it out?

This is a question I face every day. There is no single formula to determine the answer because sometimes He wants us to act and other times, to just let go! I chewed on this for a while and didn't get an answer. I read the rest of Jacob's story where he faced his brother Esau again, wrestling with the Lord, and learned to trust Him in a greater way.

Finally, the brakes screeched and God made my mind make a sharp right turn!

God wants us to know that "how we choose to be" is more important than "what we choose to do."

There is a position, posture, a frame of mind, a way of living, or a perspective we can choose that leads us to know what to do. Over and over again, Paul tells us what this position looks like.

As a prisoner for the Lord, then, I urge you to live a life worthy of the calling you have received. Be completely humble and gentle; be patient, bearing with one another in love. Make every effort to keep the unity of the Spirit through the bond of peace. – Ephesians 4:1-3

Therefore, as God's chosen people, holy and dearly loved, clothe yourselves with compassion, kindness, humility, gentleness and patience. Bear with each other and forgive one another if any of you has a grievance against someone. Forgive as the Lord forgave you. And over all these virtues put on love, which binds them all together in perfect unity.

Let the peace of Christ rule in your hearts, since as members of one body you were called to peace. And be thankful. Let the message of Christ dwell among you richly as you teach and admonish one another with all wisdom through psalms, hymns, and songs from the Spirit, singing to God with gratitude in your hearts. And whatever you do, whether in word or deed, do it all in the name of the Lord Jesus, giving thanks to God the Father through him.
– Colossians 3:12-17

But the fruit of the Spirit is love, joy, peace, forbearance, kindness, goodness, faithfulness, gentleness and self-control. Against such things there is no law.
– Galatians 5:22-23 (NIV)

He is a good Father. He will give us what we need to do – what He has called us to do. It is not through self-effort that we "create" these characteristics in our lives. It is through abiding in Him and receiving the fruit of the Spirit. We are the branches. The fruit blooms and grows on the branches. The fruit of the Spirit equips us for our purpose. The branches will never produce fruit – fulfill their purpose – unless they stay connected to the vine.

When we allow God to be our peace, to increase our love, to create patience in us, and the many other benefits of staying connected to Him, our relationships cannot help but grow in a healthy way. Our role is to continually choose this position in life. To rest in Him and stay connected to the vine – no matter what – so that the fruit of the Spirit flows through us.

I don't know about you, but when I'm stirred up like the water we've talked about before, it is very difficult to have a right mind to make decisions. However, when I have God's peace, I see more clearly. When I have love, kindness, and humility, I make very different decisions because I am not in the heat of the moment trying to protect myself. The good news is, the fruit of the Spirit comes from Him and flows through us. It is not a work of the flesh. It is an act of the Spirit.

The three-letter word "let" can change your life. When we surrender to the Lord and allow Him into our lives even when we think we're justified in holding on to something, He will redeem it in a much more beautiful way than we could have restored it ourselves. We can approach life knowing we have victory– not fighting for victory – because we have found rest through Jesus.

Although there are scriptures that say Jacob was nervous, I believe that over and over again, God revealed He was with him. It made a difference in his choices. I am so thankful God used this story to remind me of what He values. I think we get the cart before the horse. We make a big deal about what we should "do" and forget to stay connected to the vine and "be" who we are in Christ. We are called to be doers of the Word, be obedient to our call, and be the hands and feet of Jesus. In "doing" these things we will not be perfect, but God is merciful. He is with you. Just remember, before you make a decision about "what to do," take some time to seek Him about "how to be."

17

HONEST SCALES

Dishonest scales are an abomination to the L\ORD,
But a just weight is His delight. – Proverbs 11:1

When I saw this scripture, I was actually looking up another scripture and my eyes locked in on this one. I instantly knew God was showing me dishonest scales can apply to more than just money. They can also apply to people. We can be dishonest in how we judge, or even simply assess, other people. Sometimes, we do this knowingly and sometimes, we do this without realizing it.

There are times when we think we know "how" someone is because of outside indicators or our own inside emotions toward them. Recently, I went on a cruise with over 20 women from my church as a Women's Retreat. I didn't really know any of the women who attended very well. In my mind, I thought I knew "how" some of them were, based on what I could see on the outside and what I read on their Facebook posts. As we spent nine days together– two extra days thanks to Hurricane Harvey – I realized I did not make a proper assessment. It was fun to have God show me who they really were as I listened to them. It wasn't that I had a negative view of them, I had just made wrong assessments about "how" they were.

Before I continue, I need to clarify: The truth God wants us to glean here is NOT about judging people. God tells us not to do that for very good reasons. If I use the scale to weigh someone's faults against their good, I will automatically take that information and determine if they are a "good" or "bad" person. WHOA! That's not my job and I don't know everything. Everyone is a treasure. The truth God does want us to glean is about how we see others and our-selves. Please continue reading with that in mind!

There are also times when we get upset and list the faults of oth-ers. It's easy to stack one side of the scale and list the bad things they did without taking their perspective and their positive actions into consideration. The faults we find may not be true – they may only be our opinion of someone's actions. It's also easy to not consider our "part" if the situation involves us.

The opposite can be true as well. We can list all the things we did right without acknowledging what someone else did right. "I have done the dishes, the laundry, swept the floor, gone grocery shop-ping, and changed six diapers. You haven't done a thing to help me!" On the other hand, the husband may come home after a long day at work and wonder what his wife has done all day! Well, maybe it's worth taking a moment to think about what they actually do to help. It's always wisdom to assess both sides and ask God to show you the truth. If it still comes out uneven, we can ask God to give us grace to continue with a right heart. You can't take a snapshot of a moment in life to weigh, either. The Lord will help you see the bigger picture.

It's easy to become jealous of others. We can easily be led down the road of stacking a whole bunch of things against someone because of jealous feelings. Pastor Troy always says, "You see their glory, but you don't know their story." That is so true. We might see a woman who seems to have more than we think she should have. She has the shoes, the hair, the favor in ministry, and the perfect family. Many times, our minds will try to find things wrong about them to make us feel better about ourselves. On the other side of the scale are the times she went without and kept a positive attitude, she bought the shoes at a thrift store for three dollars, or somebody did her hair for free because God told them to. You never know what someone else's life is like! It's easy to stack one side of the scale against them without having the truth.

Another case where scales can be dishonest is when we outright refuse to see the truth about someone. Many people are bent toward "mercy" in their personality. While this character trait can have amazing strengths, a potential weakness of merciful people is that they tend to "give in" a lot. We should always look for the best in others but have our eyes open to what the Holy Spirit reveals about them as we walk in relationship. He will never reveal something to shame them. We can receive wisdom in how to handle situations if we allow Him to open our eyes. It can also be difficult to admit if they are taking advantage of us because we know the reason they needed to borrow that money, sleep on a couch, or borrow our car. Parents can easily do this with their own children. It's easy to look at your children and think they're just right in every way because you know them and love them the way a parent should. That doesn't mean all of their behavior is right. We should have a balanced view and the right perspective of things. Both sides of the scales come into play.

Now, let's look in the mirror. There are times when we are blind to our own faults. I know this has been true for me. There were times when I would get so upset with my husband for doing something and within 24 hours, God would show me I do the same thing. I was stacking the scale against him when I wasn't viewing myself in the same manner. **I am not talking about beating yourself up or searching for your flaws. I am talking about having an attitude of humility where you truly see things the way God does so He can help you! Anytime He shows us our own faults or the faults of others, He is ready to redeem that situation in a positive way if we let Him.**

We can also be blind to our own strengths. It's easy for me to list a bunch of things I'm not good at. I'm not good at cooking, homeschooling, staying on track sometimes – you name it! I can compare myself to others and feel like I fall short in so many areas. Would God say those things to me though? God would want me to see the other side of things and recognize my strengths even though I have weaknesses as well. He wants you and me to have a Kingdom view of ourselves and other people.

Again, there is no condemnation for those who are in Christ (Romans 8:1). It's not about looking for flaws. It's about being honest. When we are honest, we can proceed in the right direction. When we are in denial or allowing a blind spot to remain, who knows what direction we will walk?!

Humility and Meekness

I asked God to talk to me about this and I heard two words: humility and meekness. Those words came to mind so quickly and clearly that I did some research:[14]

Humility is defined in the dictionary as "freedom from pride or arrogance." Let's look at Wikipedia:

"**Humility** is the quality of being **humble**. In a religious context, this can mean a recognition of self in relation to God."

Did you get that? Humility is knowing God is God and you are not! My favorite definition is from author C.S. Lewis:

> **"Humility** is not thinking less of yourself. It is thinking of yourself less."

God says He exalts the humble (James 4:6). He also gives grace to the humble but resists the proud (Matthew 23:12). The Word also says pride comes before the fall. Do you know what comes before honor?

Wisdom's instruction is to fear the Lord,
and humility comes before honor. – Proverbs 15:33 (NIV)

If God gave us a position of honor before we had the quality of humility, we would be tempted to misuse it for our own gain. Think about King Saul. He was immediately given honor and power as the first king of Israel. He failed as King because he had no humility and couldn't take responsibility for his poor decisions. When you begin walking in humility and thinking about others the way that God does, you make very different decisions with the gifts God has given to you. King David was so humble that he did not kill Saul when he had the chance. The Lord knows a humble person like King David will follow His lead.

The dictionary defines *meekness* as "enduring injury with patience and without resentment." *Wikipedia* has this to say on the subject:

> **Meekness** is an attribute of human nature and behavior. It has been defined several ways: righteous, humble, teachable, patient under suffering, longsuffering, willing to follow Gospel teachings; an attribute of a true disciple. Meekness has been contrasted with humility as referring to behavior toward others, whereas humility refers to an attitude towards oneself. Meekness meaning restraining one's own power so as to allow room for others.

I love that simple clarification. Humility is an attitude or perspective about "yourself," where meekness refers to your behavior toward "others."

One of the best explanations of meekness I have heard is meekness is "bridled strength." Imagine a wild stallion. He is a fierce animal that can use his power to kill if he wants to. Now imagine that same stallion taken into captivity and tamed. The stallion can now be bridled, saddled, and ridden by a human. That same stallion is powerful enough to kill the human riding him, but he doesn't.

Understand I am not simply saying meekness is being able to kill someone, but you don't. It's about restraint. Sometimes, meekness is *not* taking over a project you could do very well to give someone else an opportunity to succeed. Meekness is not weakness! **Jesus is meek.**

Take my yoke upon you and learn from me, for I am gentle and humble in heart, and you will rest for your souls.
– Matthew 11:29

Jesus is kind and gentle. He IS love. Do you also remember that He turned over tables in the temple and told the Pharisees the hard truth about using the Temple – a place of prayer – as a place to steal from the people? Jesus is a great example of someone who had great power but chose to be humble in every situation.

Unfortunately, many think meekness is synonymous with being a doormat. Meekness does not mean you let people get away with whatever they want.

Recently, I listened to a message by John Hagee on the subject.[15] He said to *not* respond to a situation in which you *should* respond is not meekness. It is callous – and I would also say it can be motivated by fear. Sometimes, we hide behind meekness as an excuse to not act when God really does want us to. Remember that, if handled correctly, conflict can strengthen a relationship or situation. Conflict is not bad. We just need to handle it in the right way.

God values meekness. It is a sign of strength.

Blessed are the meek, for they will inherit the earth.
- Matthew 5:5 (NIV)

In Exodus 12:3, Moses calls himself "the meekest of men" though the New King James says, "(Now the man Moses was very humble, more than all men who were on the face of the earth.)" While meek and humble are not interchangeable, they are very similar and need to be clarified. Moses was meek, not weak! You cannot be a weak man and lead whiney, ungrateful people in the desert for that many years. It is not weak to go to God when He wants to kill them all and influence the Lord to spare them by volunteering to die with them. Moses was a powerful and meek man!

How can these two words make a difference in how you weigh life? **Perspective!**

Having meekness and humility gives us the right perspective and starting point. When we allow meekness and humility to function in our lives, we're not trying to fight for power. We're living from a position of power. We know where we stand with God and have security in that. We're not searching for our security from situations or other people. Instead, we are secure enough to see things the way He does and react accordingly. We are committed to God's plan and trust He will work it out. He will reveal the truth about situations and lead us to act in wisdom with humility and meekness.

As we get ready to receive new Christians and prepare for the great harvest, we will have plenty of opportunity to practice this. Of course, we will know more about Christianity than new people coming into the church do. It will be tempting to be offended by unchanged lifestyles, ignorance, and struggles. However, if we see them with humility and meekness, and choose to see the "God" in them and love them, we will welcome them into the body of Christ. These new people will bring gifts and talents the Body of Christ needs. We need them, and they need us. The more whole and healed we are as a body of Christ, the more we are able to receive new believers and help them in their walk. We can remember that Jesus paid the same price for them – our value is the same. He doesn't weigh us, just as we shouldn't weigh one another. Everyone is a treasure.

This may even apply to people in our lives right now. There may be someone in your life that makes it difficult because they're not where you are in your walk with God. I pray that God will help you love yourself and your brothers and sisters with humility and meekness. I pray He helps you keep the scales honest. I pray He helps you see things the way He does so you can walk in confidence.

> *But the fruit of the Spirit is love, joy, peace, patience, kindness, goodness, faithfulness, gentleness, self-control; against such things there is no law. Now those who belong to Christ Jesus have crucified the flesh with its passions and desires. If we live by the Spirit, let us also walk by the Spirit. Let us not become boastful, challenging one another, envy in one another.*
> *– Galatians 6:22-26*

18

OVERCOMING JEALOUSY

I was looking for a DVD and found an audio lesson about jealousy a friend had given me years ago. It was titled "The Spirit of Jealousy" by Arthur Burk[16] of Sapphire Leadership Group. I didn't remember listening to it. For some reason, I popped it in the CD player. This was one of those *coincidences* that can be explained as "God put that there just for me." Several things made this message completely relevant to me. Much of this chapter is inspired by that message.

Jealousy. The word does not conjure up good thoughts. I have to admit, someone being jealous of me can feel like a marker of success. Perhaps it is. It's great to have something so good, someone else wants it too. However, it shouldn't be our goal to make people jealous in a vindictive way. If it is, we need a "heart check."

We are not talking about the biblically permitted "provoke to jealousy" situation as described in the book of Romans regarding the unbelievng Jews being jealous of the believing Gentiles. This chapter is about partnering with a *spirit of jealousy* that has no desire to lead us to the Lord in any way.

When the Lord leads me to teach on something, He lets me learn it hard-core before I deliver it. I think it's His way to make sure the teaching is humble. It's mercy that leads me to greater freedom. I have had to look at some very ugly places in my life that needed to be given to the Lord. I just want you to know, I am processing this *with* you. I have not *arrived* at my destination. We all need the Lord's help. We are all in need of a Savior and fall short of the glory of God. The good news is, we have a Savior who is willing to help us.

What Is Jealousy?

Jealousy is the feeling of anger or envy when you believe someone else has an advantage. As a result, they have something or someone you want. It's those times someone walks into the room and your eyes quickly scan them and you think, "I wish I looked that good in my jeans. Must be nice to have those shoes and that good-looking guy holding your hand. What did she do to deserve him?" How about "Why does he get that car and I don't?" or "Why did he get that promotion? I've been working my butt off for ten years!" It's times you believe you deserve something and someone else did not. It's when we think, "It's not fair!" That is jealousy.

It's easy to fall into that trap without realizing it. Social media has made envy even easier. I'll be honest. There have been times I've had to put my phone down and not look at Facebook. I don't want to see vacation pictures. I don't want to see someone on date night when I haven't had one in three months. I don't want to see someone bought a new house when we're barely making ends meet. I need to manage me and not put something in front of me that's going to tempt me to become jealous.

It isn't always social media. Sometimes it happens with family. You go to your family reunion and your cousin has the spouse, the dog, the perfect kids, the perfect car, and your mom wants to tell you all about how perfect she is.

Our minds begin to wonder what we *didn't* do that they *did*. Ouch! We may feel like we have done enough to deserve it too or perhaps feel like we deserve it and they don't. I don't know about you, but that way of thinking leads me into hopelessness.

Learning to Trust Him More

Jealousy can sneak into your life in so many different ways. Recently, I asked God if there were areas in my life I wasn't letting Him in. His response was, "In your dreams. You're not asking Me for those big dreams that you dream of."

I had gotten to a place in life where I was trying to do the best with what I had instead of believing God to give me more. I decided I was going to talk to God about my dreams. There were three specific things on my heart. One of my desires was to have a closet full of new clothes. I was standing in my closet trying to find something to wear and I told God my clothes were falling apart, some didn't fit right, and many had been given to me but they just weren't my style. I began to thank the Lord that someday I would have brand-new clothes and feel good about the wardrobe choices I had. Everyone wants to feel confident in what they have on!

The next day, we went to a friend's house for lunch. The husband asked, "Did she show you show you what I got her the other day? It's the first time I've ever done something like that!" They led me to her closet where they showed me all of the new clothes he had bought her. The price tags were still on them. Her closet was organized, full of beautiful clothes that actually fit her and weren't falling apart. I was stunned. I had just finished telling the Lord I wanted that very thing and now I was standing in some other woman's closet because she had received what I wanted.

A few days later, I had to watch someone receive exactly the recognition I had prayed for. Then, I talked to the Lord about a desire to lead a certain song at church again. We went to a worship gathering and I heard my friend singing that very same song. What?!? This was the third time I prayed something very specific and had seen someone else receive it.

God was teaching me a lesson in a way that would make sense to me. By the third time, I began to thank the Lord for opportunities to trust Him with "me." I realized His heart is to make sure I am in a position to trust Him to give me what I need when it's time. The Word of God says we should "be content with what we have." If I look on the other side of the fence and think the grass is greener, I am not appreciating what God has given me. The word is very clear: God does not want jealousy or envy in our lives.

"Love is patient, love is kind, it does not envy ..."
– 1 Corinthians 13:4

*Let us walk properly as in the daytime, not in orgies and drunkenness, not in sexual immorality and sensuality, not in quarreling and **Jealousy**. – Romans 13:13*

*...for you are still of the flesh. For while there is **Jealousy** and strife among you, are you not of the flesh and behaving only in a human way? – 1 Corinthians 3:3*

When we are content with what we have, we don't feel the need to be jealous of what someone else has. The Apostle Paul was able to trust the Lord with his life. He learned how to be content when He had much and content when he had little.

Not that I am speaking of being in need, for I have learned in whatever situation I am to be content. – Philippians 4:11

When we feel dissatisfied, we are prone to be jealous of those who appear satisfied. You may never even meet the people you're jealous of like a movie star or somebody on the stage at church you've never met. You don't have to know someone to be jealous of them. Still, partnering with the spirit of jealousy can be destructive to them and you.

A Jealous Enemy

Satan is very jealous of God. The Word tells us he wanted the attention God received for himself. He still does. That's why he hates when we worship the Lord. He wants that worship. His jealousy led him to fall from the position God created him to have. His jealousy drives him to tempt us into partnering with him instead of God. Isn't that what happened in the garden of Eden?

Satan led Eve to believe he knew more than God and she should change her way of thinking to line up with his. He also walked into heaven and told God Job only worshiped him because God rewarded him. Satan tempted Job to turn from God when the circumstances in his life changed. Job didn't fall for the bait.

This may surprise you, but Satan is also very jealous of us. We have God's attention, gifts and promises and he doesn't like that at all. The Lord also put His Holy Spirit in us to make us sons and daughters – actual family that looks and acts like our Heavenly Father. Angels are God's servants – not His family. So, it should be very obvious that he is a jealous devil.

If you read the end of the Bible, you realize no matter how many people turn to him, he is still after the few that remain loyal to the Lord. This jealousy will ultimately lead him to his destruction.

"For our struggle is not against flesh and blood, but against the rulers, against the authorities, against the powers of this dark world and against the spiritual forces of evil in the heavenly realms." – Ephesians 6:12

We need to remember that. Jealousy is a spirit that tempts us to partner with it in the destruction of relationships. When a conflict arises, remember, we don't fight against flesh and blood. Something else is at work. We need to fight with the right battles with the right weapons. When we partner with jealousy, we partner with Satan's plan for that person and for us. It's *that* serious. Thoughts are huge in our fight with the enemy. We *can* take every thought captive through trusting Jesus and submitting to Him.

The Family Table

God gave me a vision of my kitchen table. There were the four places for Kevin, Andrew, Jade, and me. The Lord was talking to me about how there is no displacement at the family table. Displacement can be the root of jealousy.

Displacement is when something "takes the place" of what used to be there. It occupies space that was previously occupied by something or someone else.

Imagine a claw-foot bathtub filled with water to the very top. If wind were to blow, the water would spill over. Now imagine a 500-pound grizzly bear getting in that tub. Is the water going to stay in the tub? No. He's going to *displace* that water. He will occupy the space in the tub *instead* of the water.

There are four people in my family. There are four places set at the kitchen table. One place is set for Jade and has everything she likes and needs on it. It was created for her. No one can take her place because she is in our family and no one can be Jade but Jade. There is no chance of displacement in our family. The place is set for her just like the place is set for you at God's table. You are loved, accepted, and uniquely made. No one can be you in the kingdom but you. There is no fear of displacement because you are His. This understanding is a weapon against jealousy. My identity and my place in His family is secure. I don't care who else is at the table because they will never take my place or take what was meant for me.

I believe in having phrases or scriptures to displace thoughts that don't line up with what God says. One of my weapons against jealousy is this phrase:

"I don't want part of what He has for someone else. I want ALL of what He has for me."

I say that to myself all the time. When I walk through a house that's much nicer than mine, I say, "I don't want part of what they have. I want all of what He has for me." I'm not going to grab someone else's plate at the table and yell, "I want some of that, too!" I can trust Him to give me what I need at the right time.

Different Seasons

Blessed is the man
Who walks not in the counsel of the ungodly,
Nor stands in the path of sinners,
Nor sits in the seat of the scornful;
But his delight is in the law of the Lord,
And in His law he meditates day and night.
He shall be like a tree
Planted by the rivers of water,
That brings forth its fruit in its season,
Whose leaf also shall not wither;
And whatever he does shall prosper.

– Psalm 1:1-3

Not all trees blossom at the same time. Apple, orange, and fig trees each have their season. All trees have their season. They're all in process, but they aren't all going to bloom at the same time. Your tree *will* bloom. It's very easy to look at someone else's tree that's blooming, then look at yours when it's bare and looks like it's going to die tomorrow and be jealous. Your season will come. Your Father knows exactly when that season needs to be. You can trust Him that you will be prepared when you partner with Him. If you didn't go through the process, you wouldn't be able to bloom.

I had already been studying this when I was at my mom's house. She was telling me about two of the trees in her yard. When she started talking about trees, I started listening because I thought God may be talking to me! My grandfather had planted these two trees and she didn't know what they were because they hadn't bloomed. They hadn't had any fruit yet for her to know. She said it'd been three years and they'd never had any fruit. I asked her why. She said the conditions just weren't right; there were freezes or the weather was wrong. I asked whether they could bear fruit in the future and she said "yes," but all of those conditions had to be right for that to happen.

This conversation started me thinking. There are times I thought I should've bloomed, but I didn't. I probably have more seasons that fit in that category than times I feel like I've bloomed. There's a sovereign purpose in that, though. Within God's sovereign plan sometimes A+B does NOT equal C. Maybe what I *thought* was happening wasn't God's sovereign plan. I can still trust the Lord because He has my place set at the table and He knows exactly what I need and when.

A Shield of Honor

Even if you come to terms with jealousy in your own life, it's likely that people will still be jealous of you. That's just a human thing. What do you do when people are jealous of you? Arthur Burk shared that you need a shield of honor made up of people around you that see the Jesus in you. They remind you of who you are when you feel like you have no idea anymore. They remind you of your gifts and talents and lift you up when you're really not feeling it.

What do shields do? They protect. This is one reason we need to be connected as the Body of Christ. We need protection. Have you ever seen the movie "Gladiator?" In the arena, if one person was out there on his own he was going to die. Because they all used their shields *together* they were protected. That's how we're supposed to be. We're supposed to be that shield that protects one another.

The same is true in nature. Predators attack the animal who is isolated – not the one surrounded by others. There are times we need to be alone but be aware the devil's strategies. He likes to isolate and attack.

A Higher Perspective

Ask God to help you see people the way He does. I wish I did this every time, but when I know that someone has an insecurity and they are treating me with jealousy or anger, I pray for God to show me how He sees that person. When I pray this, sometimes I have a "Wizard of Oz" experience. You know how the "Wizard of Oz" was big, boisterous, and intimidating but when they pulled back the curtain, he was just a little man? Sometimes He shows me that person is really just hurting. He'll help me have compassion for them.

We have a secret weapon called the Holy Spirit and He will lead us into truth. God will show you how to be a shield of honor for those who are jealous of you. I know that sounds backward, but when someone is jealous of you and you start building them up, it stops the spirit of jealousy. It's going to be hard for them to continue to be jealous of you if you're the one building them up. God can show you the Jesus in them. This has also happened to me at times when I felt jealous of someone else. If I ask God to show me who they are in their heart, He usually shows me the Jesus part – His Spirit at work in them. Who am I to be jealous of the Jesus in somebody? We just have to remember we *are* the Body of Christ and we need the Jesus part in us to succeed so we can function together as we're supposed to.

Now that we know our place in the family of God is secure no matter what, there is something else that we need to discuss...

Our Assignment in the Kingdom

Each of us has an assignment and we need to be prepared for it. The worship leader is not going to let some guy get up and play guitar if he's not good at playing guitar. He will love him, he will always be his brother in Christ, he will always be safe and secure in the family of God, but he's not going to let him play on the worship team. To do that, he has to be prepared for the assignment God has given him. This applies to everything. What if you are assigned to be the CEO of a company, a police officer, or the head of a ministry? Any type of leadership position requires training.

Jealousy is not something we want to partner with. Jealousy is also very sneaky. It can enter our lives in ways we may not even recognize. Arthur Burk exposes three areas where we may be tempted to partner with jealousy. I found these to be extremely helpful points and I have added more explanation of my own.

1. Not Being Willing to Pay the Price

We see this in the story of Cain and Abel. Both brothers brought a sacrifice to the Lord. Abel's sacrifice was accepted but Cain's was not. We know God made it clear what His requirements were for the sacrifice they were to bring. The Lord doesn't play games with us. He is not a God of confusion. So, Cain knew God's expectations. Somewhere along the line, Cain decided he knew better than God and brought an insufficient sacrifice. Cain could have chosen to do what he was supposed to and offer the correct sacrifice to the Lord, but he refused to pay the price he needed to pay. It was more than likely a matter of the heart that did not please God. Cain's jealousy led him to murder his brother Abel.

While Jesus was our ultimate sacrifice, we are still called to partner with the Lord for the things He has for our lives. If we decide we are not willing to partner with the things He leads us to, we should not be jealous of the people who have what we want. It's like Pastor Troy always says, "You see their glory, but you don't know their story."

The guy who never practices and wants a spot on the worship team has no business being jealous of the guy who puts in hours of practice to be better. Most of the people God has placed in leadership have acted in obedience for the specific things God has shown them to do. God exalts the humble (Matthew 23:12). Humble people submit to the Lord. We cannot skip that step. Submitting to the Lord looks different for every person. The process He will lead *you* through to get to a certain position is different than the process He will lead others through. We have to be willing to pay the price. The price of the process is what prepares us for the purpose.

2. Insecurity about a Position You Already Have

We see this in King Saul. Saul was called to be king three times. The third time, he decided to listen, but he never felt secure in that position. When little David came along, Saul was very threatened. The Word says David was not willing to lay a hand on God's chosen king, so David was *not* a threat to the throne. Yet Saul was so consumed by that insecurity, it led him down a terrible path of self-destruction.

I was watching a show and there was a woman who said she needed plastic surgery because her fiancé was so good-looking. We know by her words that she feared someone better looking was going to take him away from her. It consumed her mind and she became somebody different. She was acting jealous toward people who didn't even exist. Have you ever known someone who become popular or successful and you think to yourself, "His life is so different now, our friendship isn't going to last. He's not going to like me or hang out with me anymore." You sabotage the relationship because you're insecure instead of resting in the fact that you already built a friendship!

3. God's Sovereignty

As strange as it may sound, God's sovereignty can cause jealousy if we don't have the right perspective. God is God. He does what He *knows* to be right. His ways are not our ways and His thoughts are not our thoughts. There are things that happen in life that you aren't expecting.

There are times God calls you to do something and you put your blood, sweat and tears into it. Then He calls you away right before the big break occurs. It can be extremely difficult to see someone else put in the position to receive the harvest you have been toiling to achieve. The truth is, that is actually what God had planned to do all along. It's not a punishment that you plowed the land and someone else reaped the harvest. It's simply what He planned to do for His sovereign purposes.

Remember the story in Matthew 20 about the vineyard owner? He hired some workers at the beginning, some at the middle, and some at the end of the day. When he began to pay everybody for their day's work, the people hired in the beginning were upset that they were all paid the same. The vineyard owner was like, "Didn't you agree to work for this amount? Isn't this *my* money? Don't I have the right to do whatever I want to do?" In God's sovereignty people will get elevated who don't appear to have paid the same price. Sometimes people get put in a position we don't think they are ready for but God's like, "Nope. We're going to do this *now!*" You and I are not God. We don't know everything and it's not our place to question His sovereignty.

I've experienced both sides of this coin. Your place in the **family** *never* changes. Your **assignment** in the Kingdom is sometimes a relay. So, you run your leg of the race as best as you can. When it's time to pass the baton, *pass* the baton. God knows the next thing He's calling you to. There may be times when the baton should have been passed to you and it wasn't, because someone else made a wrong choice. I know this is hard. It's not fair and it's not okay. These situations challenge you to trust the Lord even more. If the baton doesn't get passed to you for whatever reason, choose to trust that God knows everything and He'll work it out because He is faithful. We can trust Him. Your *knowing* of the Lord, not just your knowledge, tells you He's a good Father and you can trust His plan and His ways for you.

I have personally had to experience the baton being passed to someone else and it is very difficult to handle if you have the wrong perspective. When we realize that we're doing everything as "unto the Lord" and we are trusting in His sovereign plan for our lives, we can be comforted there is a bigger picture than we realize at work.

Your tree will bloom!

And whatever you do, do it heartily, as to the Lord and not to men, knowing that from the Lord you will receive the reward of the inheritance; for you serve the Lord Christ.
– Colossians 3:23-25

When we see others prosper, it's tempting to think, "They don't deserve that." Ask yourself, *"Have I ever had God give me something that I don't deserve?"* The answer would be yes. Have you ever been put in a job you didn't have the qualifications for? Have you been given a gift you didn't pay for? Someone may have paved the way for you and you have actually been chosen to receive the harvest. It can go both ways!

A Tale of Two Gutters

We've talked about ways we can knowingly or unknowingly partner with the spirit of jealousy. Those are places we need to be intentional about partnering with God. Arthur Burk uses the analogy of the gutters on either side of a bowling alley to explain the spirit of pride.

The first gutter is pride. Pride is when someone gets their identity through what they have or do instead of from the Lord. Pride is dangerous. It can sneak in very easily. I remember a while back when I returned to ministry. I was washing my hands and God told me, "Don't get your identity from how I choose to use you." If I can remember the exact thing I was doing when God spoke to me, it is very significant. It was a warning He was going to begin doing more in my life and He did not want me to get sidetracked by pride.

Years ago, I *did* get my identity from how He chose to use me. If I sang a song, I would do it well, so everyone would tell me I did it well. If I organized something, I wanted everyone to know I did it. Now I understand it's *"as unto the Lord,"* not because I need affirmation and encouragement from other people. Those things are wonderful, but our identity shouldn't rely on it. If I get my identity from those things instead of the Lord, I need more and more to satisfy me. Receiving man's approval becomes my focus, drive, and motivation instead of doing things as unto the Lord.

Remember the story in Luke when the disciples were so excited because the demons submitted to them when they prayed in Jesus' name? Jesus did agree that demons submitting to them was a good thing, but he also said:

> *"However, do not rejoice that the spirits submit to you, but rejoice that your names are written in heaven."*
> *– Luke 10:20 (NIV)*

Jesus reminds us not to take pride in our authority, position, or giftings, but only in Him. Our identity is supposed to come from our relationship with the Father. If we are grounded in that understanding, the Lord can open up all kinds of doors for us. Our identity is not wrapped up in those things. We will not be tempted by the enemy but will hear the voice of the Good Shepherd who is leading us. If you find your identity in the Lord, you know who you are, and you can be secure in Him. You can celebrate others without feeling threatened or jealous.

The other gutter is false humility. False humility is when you devalue or diminish your giftings and your calling. If you know God has called you to do something yet you refuse to step into it (even though you know God has equipped you), this can fall into the category of false humility. Many times, people are just trying to be nice. They may not say anything or offer assistance when they are fully capable of doing so. Or, they are waiting to be "placed" in a position that they have been longing for when God wants them to "pursue" it.

We have to understand that God does not want us to seek our own honor. Proverbs is very clear that we should not do that. However, when God does put us in a position to receive authority, or any place in his kingdom, that he has called us to we need to be willing to receive it! Jesus stood up to people when they questioned who he was. He never fell into false humility. He also taught the disciples not to do that either. He told them to go into the cities and if they were not received with honor, to leave and shake the dust off their feet. They were not allowed to tolerate a dishonor of their anointing. Neither are you. Remember the story about being seated at a wedding feast? Jesus told this parable in Luke 14. He said when you go to the wedding feast don't take the best seat because you might be demoted. That is the pride side. Then he added:

> "But when you are invited, take the lowest place, so that when your host comes, he will say to you, 'Friend, move up to a better place.' Then you will be honored in the presence of all the other guests. For all those who exalt themselves will be humbled, and those who humble themselves will be exalted."
> – Luke 14:10-11

Recently, I was at a prophetic meeting. Kevin went forward to give the offering and I was sitting in my chair thinking to myself, "It's good that he can represent our family." Then the Lord said, "Go take your place and stand next to him." What? I didn't understand. As I soon as I walked up and stood next to Kevin, God said, "This is the New Covenant." It was a revelation I needed for myself. Instead of Kevin just going to receive for our family, I am now able, empowered, and expected to receive from the Lord for myself. I needed to take my place. Shortly after that, I was standing behind someone during worship and a big area cleared in front of me. I thought, "I should move forward because I love being close to the stage where I won't get distracted!" Then I convinced myself just to stay where I was. The Lord said again, "Take your place." There are times the Lord will open up an opportunity before you but it's your job to step into it. False humility will always keep you from doing that. It's not boasting in yourself or having confidence in the flesh. It's believing who He says you are!

The disciples were told to accept the honor if others offered it and you should too. How does this relate to jealousy?

If I deny who I am in Christ and someone else accepts who they are in Christ, they may be promoted, and I can become jealous of who they are. Perhaps you were actually supposed to have that position, but you did not step into it. I am not talking about promoting yourself. I am talking about humbly stepping into what God has for you! You can actually set yourself up to be jealous if you practice false humility in your life.

True humility means we are confident in the Lord. Our confidence comes from what Jesus did.

I'm not going to look at myself and be confident. I'm going to look at Him. I'm not going to look at Him and be insecure and shrink back. I'm going to look at Him declare if, "God is for me. Who can be against Me?" I need to be confident because I don't do any good for the Kingdom if I'm not.

The book of Hebrews tells us we are not to be a people who shrink back. He tells us we can't shrink back. If God says to retreat for a while that's one thing, but if we're shrinking back out of insecurity and fear – or we're letting someone else take something that was ours, we're not going to gain anything.

His plan is big. We might not understand every part of it, but if we just do what He shows us to do, He is faithful and it's going to work out for our good. If I'm going to sit at the table, I'm going to welcome the others at the table. I'm not going to be jealous of them. They are my brothers and sisters. The truth is – and King David saw this – the wicked prosper and that doesn't make any sense to us. That's also God's sovereignty. The Bible says it rains on the just and the unjust. He has a plan for everything. We have to trust that we are secure in Him. We don't have to fight for our place at the table. Live your life *from* that place of security in Him. Kick out the spirit of jealousy!

God's love is simple and it's pure. It's crazy to think that sometimes we just don't receive it. Don't worry about what somebody else has and what you don't. Just stay focused on your loving Heavenly Father and He will give you everything you need. He has perfect plans for you. Your place at the table is secure. No one can take your place.

19

FAMILY

Sometimes when I ask the Lord what He wants me talk about in a meeting, He'll just give me one word and I have to go, "Okay, can You tell me some more about that?" Recently, I heard the word 'family' so clearly and little by little these pieces came together.

One of my daily prayers is, "Lord, help me to see this the way You do. Help me see this person the way You do." If I see circumstances and people through His eyes, I react differently and I so need the Lord to do that for me.

Recently, I was listening to Pastor Troy speak; he talked about the mind of Christ as a weapon and he read these scriptures:

Therefore, since Christ suffered for us in the flesh, arm yourselves also with the same mind, for he who has suffered in the flesh has ceased from sin, that he no longer should live the rest of his time in the flesh for the lusts of men, but for the will of God. – 1 Peter 4:1-2

Let this mind be in you which was also in Christ Jesus. – Philippians 2:5

Immediately, I had this moment where I knew, "That's what I've been praying for all these years when I prayed to 'see' the way He does." I was actually praying to have the mind of Christ.

Jesus' whole mission here on earth was to reconcile us to the Father. He gave us a picture of the Father. He said that if you'd seen Him, you'd seen the Father. From this, we understand that everything is centered around the Father. We have a perfect heavenly Father. Because we have a perfect heavenly Father, we need to let God define family and not lean on our own understanding of family based on our own experiences. God defines family. His Word will help understand His definition.

Now, here's the deal with that: all of us probably fit in the category of having had bad experiences with family – either growing up or after you grew up. You and I have also seen dysfunctional families or have been in a situation where family was the most hurtful thing for you. I'm sorry for those hurtful experiences and so is the Lord. Don't let them keep you stuck. Let God define family because He does not see things the way we do. You have to have the mind of Christ to really understand family the way that God wants you to.

Let God Define Family

Let's take a moment to get our minds set to that place where we're going to let Him define family for us.

Lord, I come to You and say that I want the mind of Christ. I thank you that Your word says I have the mind of Christ. I receive it in Jesus' name. I renounce any ungodly beliefs, strongholds, or wrong ways of thinking that don't line up with what You say about family. I choose to believe what You say about family. I pray, Holy Spirit, that You would heal family wounds in me. I command my soul (mind, will and emotions) to submit to my Spirit. I receive Your definition of family in Jesus' name. Amen.

1. You Always Have a Place in God's Family

When you choose Jesus, He chooses you forever. You always have a place at His table. Remember the family table from the jealousy chapter? You don't have to be jealous of somebody else's place because when you're in God's family, you have a place *just for you*. He has a place set just for you and nobody will ever sit in your chair.

2. There Is No Revolution in a Family

For instance, I can't say, "Well, Kevin's not doing a very good job. I think someday soon I'm going to be better than him and I'm going to become the husband." That would not work, right? It doesn't happen like that. And my daughter, Jade, can't say, "Well, I don't like being the girl in this family. I'm going to grow up and I'm going to become the son." Of course, she can't do that. She will always be the daughter. I will always be the mom. Our roles in the family are ours alone. There is so much security once you embrace your God-given role. The Prodigal Son story helps us understand this so well.

The prodigal son was living and eating with the pigs. He had left his family and thought, "Man, even the servants in my father's house eat better than this." He wasn't thinking of himself as a son anymore, was he? When he came back home, he was thinking, "Well, maybe I'll be okay enough to be a servant and I'll get to eat like them." That's not what the father did. The father received him and put him right back into standing as a son. His position never changed in his father's eyes. No matter what, he was always the son. You are always His son or daughter even on your worst days when you feel like you have totally messed up. When you have received Jesus as your Savior, you're His and that is safe and secure. Your place in the family will never change.

Why won't it ever change? It's not because we're good enough or holding our own. That's impossible. It will never change because of what Jesus did for us. This is a foundational truth you will need every day as a child of God.

I have a question for you. Who is responsible for the fall of man and bringing the curse upon man? Who sinned to create that curse? Adam and Eve, right? So, the responsibility of sin fell on Adam. We believe one man was powerful enough to bring that curse on man, right? We also need to know and believe with all of our hearts that because of one man's righteous act, because of what your Savior did for you, that curse is gone. **You no longer live under the curse.**

For if, by the trespass of the one man, death reigned through that one man, how much more will those who receive God's abundant provision of grace and of the gift of righteousness reign in life through the one man, Jesus Christ!

Consequently, just as one trespass resulted in condemnation for all people, so also one righteous act resulted in justification and life for all people. For just as through the disobedience of the one man the many were made sinners, so also through the obedience of the one man the many will be made righteous. – Romans 5:17-19 (NIV)

What Jesus did for us made us righteous forever. That's a word that seems complicated, but it has a very simple and powerful meaning. It means we have "right standing" with God. There is nothing owed, nothing unfinished. There is nothing preventing us from being seen as perfect in His sight and receiving His perfect love because we are in Christ.

And you, being dead in your trespasses and the uncircumcision of your flesh, He has made alive together with Him, having forgiven you all trespasses. – Colossians 2:13

I know that we say we are forgiven, but sometimes we don't *walk* like we're forgiven. We still carry that weight. We need to fully receive forgiveness because of what Jesus did for us so we can live like we are forgiven – because *WE ARE*! Our place in the family is not because we earned it, it's because He earned it and we chose Him. That's why.

3. Family Serves

Our Savior served in the greatest way possible. He gave His life.

"...just as the Son of Man did not come to be served, but to serve, and to give His life a ransom for many."
– Matthew 20:28 (NKJV)

Jesus also gave us an incredible example of serving when He washed the feet of the disciples. Let's be real here. Their feet were dirty! It was not like they had nice socks and shoes on as they were walking long distances through the sand and the dirt. Washing the feet was a servant's job, not the master's job. But our Savior knelt down, humbled Himself, and began to serve by washing their feet.

Have any of you ever had your feet washed before? Let me tell you, it's the weirdest thing. It's the strangest thing to have someone pick up your foot and wash it. It seems out of place and catches you off guard. The washing of your feet seems like a silly, strange thing, but it's actually a very humbling experience. It's incredible.

Let's look at a modern-day example of this point. Our son is 15 and we frequently have a lot of young guys at our house. When they come over, I don't say, "Come do the dishes" or "Did you do your laundry today?" I don't go to his friends and say, "Can you sweep the front porch and mow the yard?" I don't do that.

When you have a guest in your home, they may help you but not with daily chores or family things. Think about it this way: isn't that what creates a family? When my kids ask, "Why do I have to do that?" I always respond, "Because we're a family and families help one another."

Sometimes, we're going to give and not get anything out of it. Still, family serves. The book of Philippians talks about putting people above yourself and being humble. Serving is the way you act that out. If I really love you, I'm going to help you. Why? Family serves, but it's relationship *before* function. Because of our relationship we *want* to serve and there's a blessing in serving. Just like that, the body of Christ is a family. We are connected and called to serve one another.

4. Family Celebrates

This happens when you know your place in the family of God. When the prodigal son came home, the father was not beating him down. Instead, he came running. Read this story of their reunion:

> *"And he arose and came to his father. But when he was still a great way off, his father saw him and had compassion, and ran and fell on his neck and kissed him. And the son said to him, 'Father, I have sinned against heaven and in your sight, and am no longer worthy to be called your son.' "But the father said to his servants, 'Bring out the best robe and put it on him and put a ring on his hand and sandals on his feet. And bring the fatted calf here and kill it and let us eat and be merry; for this my son was dead and is alive again; he was lost and is found.' And they began to be merry." – Luke 15:20-24 (NKJV)*

He celebrated that his son was home. That's what God does. He celebrates you. I have a picture on my refrigerator from my daughter. She made it and put it on the refrigerator herself. How did she know to do that? Because for years she would come to me with a picture and I would tell her it was beautiful and I would put it on the refrigerator. Now, she doesn't even show me anymore. I just find them on the fridge. I love that because that means she knows she is celebrated. She knows that what she does is valued, important, and recognized.

We all need that. We all need recognition and affirmation. There's nothing wrong with that. As much as I need it, there are days when it's hard to receive that from the Lord because I'm thinking about things I've been through. I'm thinking about the mistakes instead of all the things I do right. My thinking prevents me from receiving.

You Are Celebrated

Here's the bottom line: He celebrates you because He celebrates you. Of course, your Heavenly Father wants you to have victory in this life, but He doesn't wait to celebrate you until you get it right. He always celebrates you because you are His! He sees you. He sees you as perfected because you are hidden in Christ and He sees His Son. I'm not saying that the things that are holding you back in life should remain there because God celebrates you. Knowing you're celebrated and loved will fuel you to make those changes. Don't do it backwards. We live in an upside down kingdom. Don't feel like you have to do all these things so that you can be celebrated. Do all those things because you're celebrated.

Put your dreams and accomplishments on the refrigerator. Even if it's something you haven't done yet that you have a vision for. If you've received a prophetic word, grab that, put it somewhere, and declare it. Call things as if they are, even if they're not yet. Speak it as though it has already been done. Celebrate those things. Celebrate you. God is speaking to you and He's going to show you things that you're good at, what He sees in you, and the things that He celebrates because you are worth celebrating. You need to remember that!

5. You Belong in Family

Unfortunately, you can be sitting at the family table and feel like an outsider. You're a part of the family, but you don't feel like you are. Many times, that's because the condition of your heart is not that of a son, but of an orphan.

There may be moments when you feel like you don't really belong to the family, but you *do* belong. Don't let your feelings deceive you. Your place cannot ever be taken away. There are probably places in your heart that were affected in ways that you didn't realize. Those wounds are causing you to live your Christian life – in the family of God – as if you are an orphan. You are a son (ladies too) no matter what you may think, feel or experience. The chart on the following page will help you find the places the Lord is ready to heal.[17] When you read through this chart you may find that sometimes you fit on the orphan side and sometimes you fit on the son side. That's completely normal. Don't be alarmed if you identify with some of the characteristics of an orphan. It just means God wants to reveal the Father's heart toward you in those areas. An orphan heart is not a spirit that needs to be cast out. The Father's love, and receiving it, has to *displace* that orphan heart. You have to put in something greater that causes your mind to think differently. Let the Holy Spirit do that work in you.

Family serves. But if you feel like you're not part of the family and you have an orphan's heart, then you're guarded and very conditional with other people. You may judge other people's performance and it will change the way you react to them. Or you may only view others as a way to get your own needs met. Instead of being loving and kind to someone, you're constantly thinking about yourself and what you need. You're not receiving the good and the joy you could be because that orphan heart is putting yourself first and crying, "Me. Mine. I need."

Let me give you a warning: after you read the description of an orphan heart, you will not only see characteristics of it in yourself, you'll see them in those around you. Just pray for them.

THE HEART OF AN ORPHAN		THE HEART OF SONSHIP
See God as Master	IMAGE OF GOD	See God as a loving Father
Independent / Self-reliant	DEPENDENCY	Interdependent / Acknowledges Need
Live by the Love of Law	THEOLOGY	Live by the Law of Love
Insecure / Lack peace	SECURITY	Rest and Peace
Strive for the praise, approval, and acceptance of man	NEED FOR APPROVAL	Totally accepted in God's love and justified by grace
A need for personal achievement as you seek to impress God and others, or no motivation to serve at all	MOTIVE FOR SERVICE	Service that is motivated by a deep gratitude for being unconditionally loved and accepted by God
Duty and earning God's favor or no motivation at all	MOTIVE BEHIND CHRISTIAN DISCIPLINES	Pleasure and delight
"Must" be holy to have God's favor, thus increasing a sense of shame and guilt	MOTIVE FOR PURITY	"Want to" be holy; do not want anything to hinder intimate relationship with God
Self-rejection from comparing yourself to others	SELF-IMAGE	Positive and affirmed because you know you have such value to God
Seek comfort in counterfeit affections: addictions, compulsions, escapism, busyness, hyper-religious activity	SOURCE OF COMFORT	Seek times of quietness and solitude to rest in the Father's presence and love
Competition, rivalry, and jealousy toward others' success and position	PEER RELATIONSHIPS	Humility and unity as you value others and are able to rejoice in their blessings and success
Accusation and exposure in order to make yourself look good by making others look bad	HANDLING OTHERS' FAULTS	Love covers as you seek to restore others in a spirit of love and gentleness
See authority as a source of pain; distrustful toward them and lack a heart attitude of submission	VIEW OF AUTHORITY	Respectful, honoring; you see them as ministers of God for good in your life
Difficulty receiving admonition; you must be right so you easily get your feelings hurt and close your spirit to discipline	VIEW OF ADMONITION	See the receiving of admonition as a blessing and need in your life so that your faults and weaknesses are exposed and put to death
Guarded and conditional; based upon others' performance as you seek to get your own needs met	EXPRESSION OF LOVE	Open, patient, and affectionate as you lay your life and agendas down in order to meet the needs of others
Conditional & Distant	SENSE OF GOD'S PRESENSE	Close & Intimate
Bondage	CONDITION	Liberty
Feel like a Servant/Slave	POSITION	Feel like a Son/Daughter
Spiritual ambition; the earnest desire for some spiritual achievement and distinction and the willingness to strive for it; a desire to be seen and counted among the mature.	VISION	To daily experience the Father's unconditional love and acceptance and then be sent as a representative of His love to family and others.
Fight for what you can get!	FUTURE	Sonship releases your inheritance!

Jack and Trisha Frost · Shiloh Place Ministries · www.shilohplace.org

Remember that an orphan heart needs to be displaced by the love of the Father. That love exposes the lies of the enemy so there's no place for him anymore. The truth goes in and the lie has to leave.

I was thinking of the prodigal son story and the orphan heart. The older son was really mad. He wasn't happy when his brother returned. Why? He had an orphan heart. The father told him that everything he had was his, that he didn't need to worry about what was given to his brother. Still, he didn't feel secure or know his place in the family, so he wasn't able to celebrate his brother. It's a big deal to know you belong.

My Family Forever

We attended OpenDoor Church back when they were meeting in a little building in the middle of nowhere. Now they have a much larger and nicer church building in the city that was given to them. During that time of transition for them we moved away. When we moved back five years later, I went through the New Members class just to see what was new. At the end, we were invited to join the church and were asked to sign the wall behind the stage, but I didn't do it. While I loved OpenDoor Church, at that point we had just moved back and hadn't heard clearly from the Lord where He wanted us to attend. About a year and a half later, God clearly told us to go back to OpenDoor. I jumped back in and became the interim kid's pastor.

About a year later, I was sitting in church one day and the enemy was coming at me with all these thoughts like, "You won't be at this church forever. Something might happen. You might have to go somewhere else." I was like, "Whaaaaat?" Then the thought came back to my mind that I'd never signed that wall and become a member of this church. I decided to take matters into my own hands. I went to that wall, put my name on it, and wrote, "My family forever."

I'm not saying someday I won't move and not attend OpenDoor anymore, but this *is* my family forever. The enemy was trying to cause fear and division. So many times, that is where division in the Church happens, too. You can't run away from the Body of Christ. It doesn't work. You can go from one church to another and feel like you're running away from something, but you aren't. It's all one body. We have to understand that we have a place in the family of God. It's not a place in an organization. It's the family of God. It doesn't matter what country I'm in, what church I go to, what ministry I'm in, or what I do or don't do at church. In the family of God, my place is in my *forever family*. We are called to be connected through relationship because the Body of Christ doesn't function if we aren't. We need one another!

The Lord Will Help You

God will always give you what you need to do what He has called you to do. The Lord has called us to be part of His family. He will give you the grace that you need – His empowering presence to do what you need to in your family. He will help you see them the way He does. He will give you grace to walk in the truth that you have a place in the family of God, and no one will ever be able to take that from

175

you. He will give you grace to serve even when it's inconvenient. He will give you the grace to understand that family celebrates and that you are celebrated. And He will give you the grace to have the heart of a son. He will also give you the grace to show His love to frustrating family members!

The most important thing is to remember that family always forgives over and over again just like Jesus does.

I think He's going to restructure some things in our minds. So much of how we live our lives has to do with our identity. When our identity is secure in Him, when we know that we are secure in the family of God, things may shake around us, but we are unshakeable.

20

COURAGE FROM COMMUNION

God, grant me the serenity to accept
the things I cannot change,
Courage to change the things I can,
And wisdom to know the difference.[18]

Years ago, we went to a church with a man named Ronnie. He'd been through the AA program and the Serenity Prayer was huge to him. He was a big, tall guy with a booming voice and a soft heart. He would always say, "Well Nicole, you just got to get out the Serenity Prayer and say, 'What can I change and what can I not change?'"

Now, God has to speak really simply for me to understand. One time, the Lord told me, "There are times when sorting your thoughts and feelings in your head is like trying to sort laundry *in* the basket. You can't. You have to dump it out to sort it." If you're like me, you need to be thinking about what you're thinking about and you need to realize what's going on inside of you. Dump it out of your head and figure out what you can change and what you can't. I suggest getting a piece of paper with two columns: "Things I can't change" and "Things I can change" and letting God bring clarity to you. It works!

Let's talk about the things you *can* change. These are usually the things God is calling you to change. However, in order to change you need courage. God will always give you what you need to do what He's called you to do, right? He's a good Dad. That's how we know He'll give us the courage to change the things He is asking us to change.

There are other areas of life I need to just have peace about because I can't change the circumstances. Even the areas I can't change may require a change in my thinking. You may need to put some items in both categories! Sorting things wrongly can lead to frustration just as putting a pair of bright red socks in a load of brand-new white t-shirts can lead to frustration. That frustration is *my* responsibility. It might be a sign to me that I need to reevaluate because God is asking me to change something and that's why I don't feel peace.

We do need courage to change things because life can be a little bit scary. We also need courage to persevere through change because change can be uncomfortable. It's supposed to be! One of my favorite movies is "We Bought a Zoo."[19] It is based on a true story and I learned a lot by watching the main character journey through the process of starting his life over again by taking on the responsibility of owning a zoo full of animals. Two phrases from this movie stuck with me and I still refer to them years later: "Twenty seconds of courage" and "Why not?"

When God asks us to do something, it can suddenly become very easy to come up with a lot of "why nots." We convince ourselves it wasn't the Lord, that He doesn't *really* want us to do that. Our "why nots" usually come from us predicting the future (as if we can) and determining something won't work. People won't like it or whatever other reason we find. But here's the truth: our job is to take the next step of obedience. The outcome is up to God!

Sometimes, you just need to find twenty seconds of courage to jump in, start making a mess, get started, and trust Him. Where do you find that courage? I know for sure it doesn't come from me! It comes from a different place. Here's what God spoke to me that completely blew my mind this week: **courage and communion go together.**

Sacrifices

In the Old Testament, God required sacrifices to "cover" sin. The very first sacrifice God made was for Adam and Eve to be clothed (covered) in animal skin. Under the old covenant law, there were many required sacrifices. God was very specific about how the sacrifices needed to be prepared and what needed to be sacrificed. For the sacrifice at Passover, the lamb had to be one year old and unblemished. One particular sacrifice on the Day of Atonement was made by the High Priest to cover the sins of the people for one year. The Lord would inspect the sacrifice to determine if it was sufficient. Every sacrifice and festival in the Old Testament pointed to Jesus. Then Jesus came!

Remember how I told you the Lord inspected the sacrifice to determine whether it was sufficient? This detail is important and here's why:

Examine Yourself

Therefore whoever eats this bread or drinks this cup of the Lord in an unworthy manner will be guilty of the body and blood of the Lord. But let a man examine himself, and so let him eat of the bread and drink of the cup. For he who eats and drinks in an unworthy manner eats and drinks judgment to himself, not discerning the Lord's body. For this reason many are weak and sick among you, and many sleep. For if we would judge ourselves, we would not be judged. But when we are judged, we are chastened by the Lord, that we may not be condemned with the world. – 1 Corinthians 11:27-32 (NKJV)

Scripture talks about evaluating yourself before taking communion. It says, "Do not take it unworthily." That doesn't mean I have to clean myself up before I take it. The only thing that makes me clean and pure is Him! It means I need to know about the sacrifice Jesus made for me. I need to believe it was absolutely perfect, it covered everything, and I don't have to add anything to it. Being worthy to take communion comes from knowing Jesus is worthy of my worship because He gave everything. When I choose Jesus and am now "in Christ" that means the Lord does not inspect me. He inspects the sacrifice. When God inspects the sacrifice of Jesus, it is found 100% sufficient. Praise God that's how it works!

God has not called us all to do the same thing, but He has called us all to do it the same way: by looking at Him. He is perfect. He made us righteous once and for all. We can approach the throne with boldness *because* of what He did for us; we are perfect and made righteous.

Let us therefore come boldly to the throne of grace, that we may obtain mercy and find grace to help in time of need.
– Hebrews 4:16

There are still consequences to your choices, but what you choose does not make you less righteous. Whatever you mess up on does not change your standing with God. You are righteous, which means "in right standing." Nothing can take that away because His sacrifice was perfect and covers you not for one year, but forever. He did that for you. When God looks at you, He sees His Son. You are in right-standing with Him. Any voices or thoughts that make you feel insecure are not His. Do you need to repent and change to become more like Him? Absolutely! Knowing how much someone loves you and believes in you calls you up into a better place. It's a response to perfect love! It's important to remember you are never asked to be courageous and face giants to actually *earn* your right standing with God. We can face giants *because* of our right standing with God!

True Courage

He *is* my courage. My confidence is in what Jesus has done and will do through me.

Does my courage come from thinking I have it all together? No. My courage comes from knowing Jesus did it. He was the perfect sacrifice. He covered all my sins and gives me what I need every moment. My focus is on Him. I am going to take communion worthily because I know where my true redemption came from, and it's not from me.

Why is it then, that so many times when there is something intimidating before you, you look at yourself and think, "I can't do that"? You're scared or say you're no good at that instead of looking to Him? If you know the Lord has called you to something, you need to look to Him for courage, not at yourself. That's where your courage is going to come from. If God puts a Goliath in front of you, He must know there is a David inside of you!

I had been on the worship team for a while when got a new worship pastor. He wanted to have auditions and said I needed to audition too! My place on the team was secure, but he needed to test vocal ranges. It shouldn't have been a big deal, but it was. I started to worry about it so much! I was already on the worship team and I started freaking out inside. Then God reminded me that worship isn't about me. It is about Him. Once I received that word, I was fine. After the audition, I prayed, "Thank you God for taking me through that process and letting me see the pressure is off of me. You've already taken care of this for me. If I know it's you, I'm going to have courage and step into it because You have provision for me." Why do I slap Him in the face with my insecurities? There is absolute freedom in understanding it's not about me. That's where courage comes from.

A friend just got back from a hunting trip. He was showing me a picture of a mama bear and her three cubs. At first, it just looked like a sweet picture. Then he explained it was a good thing he saw her before she saw him because she would have probably killed him to protect her cubs. That's what courage looks like when it isn't about you. It's the same courage and tenacity that Jesus had when He went to the cross *for* you!

Too many times, all the enemy has to do is get your eyes off Jesus. Just like Peter taking his eyes off Jesus while walking on the water, what did God say? We're confusing His voice with the other voices in our mind. Confusion steals our confidence. We have to know the voice of our Good Shepherd so well that nothing can compete with it. We're able to courageously say 'yes' to whatever it is He has for us, not because of us, but because of Him.

My son has this shirt that says, "Think outside the box." Jesus isn't in a box. What He's called you to do is not in a box. We don't tend to like that because boxes are safe. They have boundaries, limits, and give us excuses. What about King David? It's pretty courageous to stand in front of a giant with five stones. But he was passionate in his heart that no one was going to talk about his God in a derogatory way. That's where it came from! David wasn't looking at himself. He was looking at the Lord. In 1 Samuel 17 when David is telling Saul that he had defeated a lion and a bear, and he would defeat Goliath, he still didn't place his confidence in himself. He knew his courage came from the Lord. His courage had been tested and he knew he could trust the Lord again!

Joshua was told to be strong and courageous three times in the first nine verses of Joshua 1. He was chosen to lead the Jewish people into the Promised Land. What an awesome role to play, but it wasn't an easy one. Think about what Joshua had seen and experienced. It is certainly true he witnessed miracles like manna from heaven and the parting of the Red Sea, but he had also been a captive in Egypt. He had been sent into the Promised Land as a spy with Caleb. They saw the giants and the intimidating tribes who inhabited the land they were supposed to take. While he responded in faith by saying Israel should invade, he also heard the people not respond in faith to his report. Instead, they whined and complained. After that, Moses died. Because he went against God's word, he was not able to go into the Promised Land. Joshua didn't have a bear or a lion experience to draw from. Joshua, however, knew the Lord just like David did and just like Moses did. In fact, the Bible says he would accompany Moses to speak to the Lord and stay in the Lord's presence after Moses had left the tent. Joshua knew His power and strength. He believed the Lord and that's where his courage came from!

True courage should never come from our past experience or current abilities. Those things are not reliable. It should come from

Jesus. We should come boldly before the throne, get a word from the Lord, and trust His word as we walk in confidence toward what He has called us to.

Sometimes, looking back can build your faith. Other times, looking back can make it worse. If God asks you to move forward in something, do not look at past failures as a future expectation. Trust Him.

Let the Lord fill in those holes that make you feel incomplete and inadequate to fulfill your calling. Silence competing voices by listening only to His voice. If you can, take communion today and take it in a worthy manner because you know His sacrifice is complete. Just "knowing" what Jesus did for you is one thing. Actually knowing *Him* will take it to a whole new level. He is perfect and has perfected you in righteousness because of what *He* did. Because of what He did, you *can* be courageous.

> *God, grant me the serenity to accept*
> *the things I cannot change,*
> *Courage to change the things I can,*
> *And wisdom to know the difference.*

21

SOAR LIKE THE BUTTERFLY

A prophetic word is when God tells someone else something to tell you. It is not a man's interpretation, but rather the Father's heart for you.

> *But the one who prophesies speaks to people for their strengthening, encouraging and comfort.* – *1 Corinthians 14:3*

Sometimes, God uses messengers with "skin on" to share His heart with us through words. Many years ago, we had a visiting speaker at the church we were attending. When I went up for prayer he told me this:

"You have had some dreams that have been trampled on, but you will soar like the butterfly and see them fulfilled."

At the time, I didn't have any hopes or dreams that had come crashing down. Life wasn't easy, but it wasn't bad. I just held onto that word and it began to make more sense as I got older. The hopes and dreams in me that were probably trampled on were hopes and dreams of how life "would be," not of things I would receive or status I would attain. Really, now that I think about it, the hopes and dreams were probably all about my wish for security in life.

I have always wanted to be significant in life. Not famous – just significant. There had definitely been an attack on that. I had made enough mistakes to open the door to shame and condemnation. Often, those voices *did* make feel like I was being trampled.

So, in my interpretation of this prophetic word, I thought, "Wow, that means 'someday' all of these things will lineup and life will be easy." I literally just held onto that thinking that "someday" it would happen. *"Someday" I will be above all of this. "Someday" everybody will be happy with me. "Someday," I will have more than enough money. "Someday" I will be like one of those women that has it all together. Someday...*

I received that word in my late 20s. Fast-forward to 2015 when I was 39 years old. In between that time, we had many financial trials, struggles in our marriage, I had been diagnosed with MS, we had been wrongly accused of things which almost resulted in legal action, and we had moved many times. We had many other struggles yet somehow my faith in God always got me through the hard times. They weren't all hard days. I really believe we are supposed to live in the moment and try to see the blessing in everything. So, my attitude was "just make the best with what you have." My mom did a great job of teaching me how to do that! I cannot say I always did it with a smile, but I tried.

At this time in 2015, a friend asked me to lead a group of kids at VBS. I was really struggling with my health and was hesitant to commit. I decided to do it anyway. I hate giving the devil any satisfaction of victory by limiting my life. Many times, you commit knowing *you* don't have enough but *Jesus* does!

I was excited about the opportunity to work with kids again. When I was a public school teacher, I had a soft spot in my heart for the kids with strong personalities who were always getting into trouble. Those kids turn out to be strong leaders if you steward that energy and passion. So it was with Chris at VBS. He was such a bubbly kid. I just loved him! One time, we were in line for the restroom and he was goofing off and couldn't stand still. Talk about wiggly! I don't remember why he said this, but he just blurted out, "Butterflies lay caterpillar eggs."

An Ear to Hear

You know those times when it hits you that the Holy Spirit is speaking to you? This was one of those times. God was saying to me through Chris that "when you mature you reproduce." Since then, I have known that my efforts of seeking out wholeness and healing are not only about me, but my wholeness and victory is for others. The more whole and healed I am, the more mature I grow in Jesus, and the more equipped I am to reproduce others in the faith. I cannot stay immature, wounded, and insecure and expect to reproduce sons and daughters of the faith. That was an amazing revelation to me and I shared it at VBS with all of the kids and leaders. The next day, Chris's Aunt Kristie brought me this butterfly ring she found at the zoo. She said, "Is this weird? I just think the Lord told me to give you this ring."

Here's the crazy part: Kristie was not in the meeting where I shared what Chris said about the butterfly. She had taken her daughter to the zoo where she bought a jewelry set. It came with a necklace, bracelet, and ring. She said, "I would have chosen to give you the necklace or the bracelet, but God said to give you the ring." WHAT?!?! God speaks to us so specifically! If we listen and believe the prophetic words He brings our way, testimonies of His love are sure to follow.

As I was driving home that day, the Holy Spirit hit me again. I was looking at this sweet little ring and the Lord spoke to me. I have tears in my eyes again as I remember that moment. He said, "You can soar like a butterfly because you can choose not to let things hold you down." I know that sounds so simple, but it changed my world.

The Power to Choose

All these years, I'd been waiting for "someday" to happen. In that moment, driving down HWY I-35 I realized *someday is now!* I no longer felt the need to just make do until "someday" happened. I realized I could make choices that let me soar. I could choose not to let someone's bad attitude pull me down. I could choose not to let somebody's negative perception of me hold me in a cage. I could choose not to let my health define who I was or let the weight of this world define who God is. So much opened up to me in that moment. Now, I am not waiting for "someday." I'm trying to walk out every moment with the Lord. I am learning to soar because I *choose* the truth instead of being bound up by lies.

It's a process, and I have learned so much about becoming secure in Jesus – doing things even if I don't feel confident, being willing to make mistakes, or stand my ground for the truth no matter who is upset with me. I believe God put gifts and talents in me that He wants me to use. The same is true for you. Engage in the process of transformation just like the butterfly. At first the caterpillar eats. Be a consumer of everything Jesus! Then the caterpillar enters a cocoon. There will be times in your life when you need to get alone with God. It may be an actual time of getting away with the Lord and separating yourself from others or a time of separating your thoughts. In that "cocoon" time an incredible transformation takes place. The struggle of getting out of the cocoon is actually what builds the strength the butterfly needs to fly. Without resistance, the wings would not develop. I know we can all identify with this part of the process! It changes your perspective when you know you are on your way to freedom!

Someday is NOW! You have more power than you know to change your life because the same power that rose Jesus from the dead lives in you! It has to be said that there are definitely times and seasons for God to do specific things in our lives. Sometimes, there is a God ordained "time" for something to happen which requires a "someday."

It's Not Only about You

Remember, when you mature you can reproduce, and your victory is not just about you! It's for the people you will help along the way. So, face things in your life but CHOOSE not to let anything weigh you down. Ignoring issues in your life does not truly allow you to soar. That's called denial! The Lord wants us to bring everything to Him, do what He asks us to do and soar because we trust Him with EVERYTHING!

What does it look like to soar?

Living as Those Made Alive in Christ

Since, then, you have been raised with Christ, set your hearts on things above, where Christ is, seated at the right hand of

God. Set your minds on things above, not on earthly things. For you died, and your life is now hidden with Christ in God. When Christ, who is your life, appears, then you also will appear with him in glory.

Put to death, therefore, whatever belongs to your earthly nature: sexual immorality, impurity, lust, evil desires and greed, which is idolatry. Because of these, the wrath of God is coming. You used to walk in these ways, in the life you once lived. But now you must also rid yourselves of all such things as these: anger, rage, malice, slander, and filthy language from your lips. Do not lie to each other, since you have taken off your old self with its practices and have put on the new self, which is being renewed in knowledge in the image of its Creator. Here there is no Gentile or Jew, circumcised or uncircumcised, barbarian, Scythian, slave or free, but Christ is all, and is in all.

Therefore, as God's chosen people, holy and dearly loved, clothe yourselves with compassion, kindness, humility, gentleness and patience. Bear with each other and forgive one another if any of you has a grievance against someone. Forgive as the Lord forgave you. And over all these virtues put on love, which binds them all together in perfect unity.

Let the peace of Christ rule in your hearts, since as members of one body you were called to peace. And be thankful. Let the message of Christ dwell among you richly as you teach and admonish one another with all wisdom through psalms, hymns, and songs from the Spirit, singing to God with gratitude in your hearts. And whatever you do, whether in word or deed, do it all in the name of the Lord Jesus, giving thanks to God the Father through him. – Colossians 3 (NIV)

This passage makes it clear. What we choose to focus on steers us in life. If we choose to let God put to death the things of the flesh, we set our minds on things above, we clothe ourselves with the things of the Spirit, and we let the peace of God dwell in our hearts, we will be so Kingdom-minded, the weights of this world will have no hold on us. Again, this is a process. Unfortunately, it doesn't just get handed to us as part of our "salvation package." Learning to hear and trust God more and more with every part of our lives can be such an intimate journey. We can actually begin to enjoy the process. There will be places in life where we are soaring and other places where we are still learning.

The Word says, "Let the peace of Christ rule in your hearts..." That tells us that peace is a choice because peace is actually a person – Jesus Christ the Prince of Peace! When we give Him dominion over a place in our life where we're struggling, He can work there. Peace does not have to only occur when everything goes perfectly. We can choose peace even when we aren't getting our way. We can choose to be so heavenly minded that we become un-offendable as we trust God to work things out.

A Few Other Things about Butterflies

Butterflies lay their eggs on milkweed. Milkweed is the only plant caterpillars can eat. Butterflies also lay their eggs one at a time in a place where predators cannot find them. Butterflies set their offspring up to succeed. Secure people empower others. I have to say, I spent way too many years being insecure. While I tried to be encouraging to people, I would secretly want to find their faults, so I could think better about myself. I feel different about that now. I want to see others succeed because it's the Jesus in them at work. Why would I be jealous of that? We are all powerful in the Kingdom.

Butterflies are also sensitive to the wind. Many times, the angels and Holy Spirit show up like a wind. We want to be sensitive to the things of the Lord. God designed His children to be sensitive to Him. If we are hard, calloused, indifferent, or guarded, it is because hurt has created a layer over our hearts. God never intended for us to be that way or guard our own hearts. Philippians 4 tells us our job is to trust Him and He will guard our hearts.

I read a book one time by Stacy Eldredge, which I highly recommend. It's called *Becoming Myself.*[20] Just one sentence changed my life. She wrote, "What if becoming yourself is just being who you really were in the first place." In life, much of the journey we take is just removing the layers that life has "put over" who we really are in Christ. It's not about attaining something separate from you. It's about finding out who you are inside and letting that part out! It's realizing our hope is in Jesus – not in getting it all together or finally having everything or everyone we want. Those "good" things can quickly become idols if we aren't careful.

We all need people around us that know who God says we are. Sometimes, what you see on the outside is not going to reflect that! Just ask my husband and kids! I have a friend named Joanna who has faithfully encouraged what God has spoken about me. She knows what butterflies mean to me. She is also the best gift giver ever! She has given me so many butterfly gifts. For my 40th birthday, she gave me a butterfly necklace. I put butterflies in places to remember what God has said. Sometimes, we have to be intentional about what we look at, what we hear, what we say. Actually, not sometimes, but all of the time!

This prophetic word was not just for me. It is for all of us. You can soar like a butterfly because God made you that way – even the guys! You have to partner with Him in that process. You can be as angry, bitter, harsh, or hurt as you want to be and that is always your freedom. Love does not control. You can be saved and going to heaven, but not have victory in this life. God allows us the freedom to choose because He loves us. You can choose not to let the worries and weights of this life pull you down. You can soar like that butterfly and bring glory to your Heavenly Father.

22

PROBLEMS AND PURPOSE

I was looking for something under my bed and found this toy. I know it looks like it was probably one of my kid's toys, but it's actually mine. I have random things I use as props for messages I teach. I use this one when I talk about fitting in. However, this time, the Lord used it to speak to me about *process.*

I recently saw a video that floored me. A man was trying to fit a suitcase in an overhead bin on an airplane and it was obviously too big. While I was watching this man struggle with his spatial skills, on the top of the screen there was a picture of this toy. The caption read, "Why these toys are critical as kids." It was so funny, and it blew my mind that it was the same toy I was about to write about. It was a demonstration of the consequences of trying to skip the process!

I used to say, "I hate process." It's the reason I hate painting. You have to go buy all the stuff, tape things down, cover things up with drop cloths, and apply multiple coats. It's too many steps. I have a hard time when I know there are many steps *before* I even begin a project. As I grow older and wiser, I'm changing my mindset on process (maybe not painting). I am realizing how important the process actually is.

I have been working with a little girl who has some challenges to overcome. She has dealt with so much trauma in her short little life. She's playing catch-up on many life skills. From day one, we have been using the same puzzle to work on some of these skills. At first, she didn't even know how to get the pieces out. Once she figured out how to take them out, she knew they fit back in, but didn't know how to line up the edges to accomplish this. She would slam them down and push on them, but they weren't in the right place. After a couple of months, she learned how to do the puzzle from start to finish on her own and you could see her sense of accomplishment when she did. It was a process for her to learn to do the puzzle.

The problem begins the process that prepares you for the purpose.

When we understand that the problems we face in life really do have a purpose, it changes our perspective. If we don't understand this, we get upset that we are facing so many problems because they are getting in our way.

There are problems we bring upon ourselves because of our own choices. Some problems are not connected to anything we did or didn't do. Our hope is in the Lord no matter how the problem started. Those problems are not God's heart for us at all, but He can redeem every problem to bear fruit!

James 1 says, "My brethren, count it all joy when you fall into various trials…"

To our human minds, it doesn't make sense to have *joy* and *trials* in the same sentence. It makes perfect sense to God. Why? Because problems are supposed to produce fruit! Each problem is an opportunity to become more like Him. You can be fruitful *if* you handle them with the Lord.

Don't Bail on the Process!

However, if you quit before the purpose is complete, you have the problem and sometimes an incomplete process. When my brother, Eric, died so many people said, "Time heals. Just give it time." That is so untrue. Time doesn't heal. God does. You can stay as angry, bitter, powerless, and unforgiving as long as you want to. That's what an incomplete process looks like. If you choose not to engage with the Lord in the process, you will never produce fruit and you will feel stuck! These places can also become strongholds in our lives because we are living under the lie of defeat.

Do you know people like that? Are there places in your life like that? I know I have places in my life I don't really want touched by the Lord. For one reason or another, I am content to just deal with the problem over and over again rather than engage in the process with Him. I have the problem and the negative effects of the problem, but I have no redemption if I bail on the process or never begin. If I would engage in the process with Him, I would see fruit. The purpose of victory in that area of my life would be fulfilled. Wow! I am preaching to myself right now. The Lord is so patient with us that, in His mercy, He will give us multiple opportunities to overcome.

Have you ever noticed the same problems showing up in your life over and over again? It may not be with the same people or circumstances, but the same issues keep coming up? The same types of relationships, financial struggles, or problem that is all too familiar? Those are the opportunities I am talking about.

We think we can run away to avoid the issue, but God does not want us to have places of failure or intimidation in our lives. He gives us another chance to engage in the process and be victorious. It's not punishment. It's mercy. We are overcomers! There is no condemnation for those in Christ. Even if it takes 57 times, He celebrates our victory and He loves us the same always.

He is patient with us, so we need to be patient with ourselves and others. Don't enable. Be patient. There is a big difference. Being patient does not excuse negative behavior. Patience sees the purpose and allows room to learn as we are "in process" toward it. Ask God to help you see things the way He does. Remember the little girl and the puzzle? I could have kept her from progress if I had shamed her for not knowing how to do it right away or making mistakes. We can do that to ourselves too.

We all have many processes happening at once in our lives. Maybe we have learned how to put the star in the toy, but we have no clue how the oval works yet. Trust His process even when it's hard to understand.

Trust in the Lord with all your heart and lean not on your own understanding; In all your ways acknowledge Him, and He shall direct your paths. – Proverbs 3:5-6 (NKJV)

If you bailed on a certain process in the past, you might get to start right where you left off. More often, you get to start all over again. The Lord is perfect in His ways. You gain territory when you engage in the process and the purpose of freedom is fulfilled. Many times in my life, it looked like the same problem was cropping up, but I knew I had gained victory in that area. When you gain ground, you need to stand on it. Reminding the devil of your victories is a great way to resist him!

Therefore, submit to God. Resist the devil and he will flee from you. – James 4:7

Short Term and Long Term Processes

Some problems have a short-term purpose. Have you learned how to fix a problem and immediately you helped someone with that same problem? When that has happened to me, my fruit was extended to someone else and I was able to shorten someone else's process. I pray that you and I will recognize when our process is shortened by someone else.

I heard a story from a friend about a day he was running late to everything. He hates running late. It was hard for him to finally stop stressing out about the time. At the end of his day, he crossed paths with someone and shared the Lord with her. In God's eyes, he was actually right on time! The problem: he was running late. The process: learning to surrender his day to the Lord's timing. The purpose: to bless the woman. Isn't that awesome? God's perspective is so different from ours.

Some problems have long-term purposes that require more passion. The problem and process may be long or just intense. Problems like abuse, trauma, or long struggles take more time, effort, and emotion. Along the way, the passion to fulfill the purpose is stirred. The purpose usually isn't clear at the beginning of the process. Each step of faith makes that purpose more clear. The redeemed, healed, and victorious fruit of the process becomes part of who you are. It's a deep process.

I want to say again the Lord *did not* put problems in your life. However, the redemption of them can be amazing. Many times, people who have experienced the most pain become the biggest advocates for those still suffering. Their problem stirred a passion to solve the problem no matter what the process would be!

And we know that all things work together for good to those who love God, to those who are the called according to His purpose. – Romans 8:28

The Lord already has a purpose before He ever allows the problem to come into your life. It's His purpose. Don't fall into the trap of justifying why you don't need to engage in the process. At times, it can seem like other people are part of your process and you are waiting on them. Engage in *your* process.

You also need to know the difference between solving a problem and engaging in the process. This is all about our expectations. There may not be a happy ending even when we are completely committed to the process. Maybe the process was about helping you become more like Jesus and had nothing to do with the physical outcome. The result may be fruitful even though it appears unsuccessful. The purpose can be very different than you expect. I once dug through some trash and found real gold jewelry in the bottom. I thought the $120 I sold it for was "me money," but I gave it to a single mom who needed it. Be OK with whatever His purpose is. His ways are perfect.

There is no formula that applies to everyone and every situation. What prepares me for my purpose may not be the same thing that prepares you for the same purpose. God is the greatest parent ever and while He loves all His kiddos the same, He doesn't treat us all the same. What works for you, may not work for me and God knows that!

Sometimes Helping Doesn't Help

I was praying for a younger lady I know. She was struggling in some areas and I just wanted to jump in and help her. I knew what to do. I clearly heard the Lord say, "Don't you dare take away her process." Whoa! He said, "You have been through that process. You let her do the same." I was excited to know there was at least one process I had completed. Through this experience, I learned we can actually hinder someone from bearing fruit by taking away their process and trying to do it for them. If they don't go through the process, they will not be prepared for the purpose. I can help but I must be careful not to take away their opportunity from the Lord. The only way to navigate "how" to help is through prayer.

I love overcomer stories about people who have faced tremendous difficulty and used those same struggles to fuel the passion that leads them to their purpose. That can be you. What problems are you facing right now? Declare these truths and engage in the process. The victory is worth it.

The problem is not a hindrance it's a stepping stone.

The problem is not tearing me down it is building me up.

The problem is not holding me back it is moving me forward.

The problem begins the process that prepares me for the purpose.

In him and through faith in him we may approach God with freedom and confidence. – Ephesians 3:12 (NIV)

23

PROSPER WHERE YOU'RE PLANTED

My normal life is usually busy, but recently, it was insane! I had to pull out my calendar to remember everything I had done. It was a mixture of great things and things I needed extra grace to do. I knew in advance it would be extra busy, so I was proactive in making sure it wasn't chaotic. In the past, I've rushed through one thing to get through the next and not enjoyed any of it. I was so ready to check it off my to-do list, I forgot to take time to enjoy having dinner with people or spending time with my family. I know that sounds crazy, but I bet you do it too.

I often tell my son there will be times when you are *task oriented* and times when you are *people oriented*. I reminded him not to get them confused! If you are trying to get tasks done while you should be focusing on people, relationships suffer. If you hang out with people while you need to be accomplishing tasks, you may never get anything done.

Holding Your Breath

Sometimes, we enjoy the things on our calendar and sometimes we don't. It's human nature to want to be somewhere else if you don't like where you are. Maybe it's an actual place or a situation. Daydreaming about the future can be used as a coping mechanism to get through the day. It can also leave you feeling like you are holding your breath waiting for the next thing or waiting for God to rescue you. It's fine to hold your breath if something is going to happen in the 30 seconds, but if you hold your breath too long you cut off life to your body. The same can happen in the realm of your mind. You can miss what God is doing right now because you are longing for the future. You get so wrapped up in what's next, new, or just longing for relief from your current season in life, that you miss what God is doing this very moment.

Like I said, "holding your breath" in your mind can be harmful and lead to the death of relationships, opportunities, and blessings you didn't realize were in front of you. It's hard to realize you are doing this. It's certainly OK to be excited for the future. You should have expectation and hope of great things to come. You just need to have the right mindset. You can become very angry, bitter and resentful if you are impatient for life to be different.

The key is staying in the moment while you are hopeful for the future.

It's not wrong to want things to change for the better. There is probably something in your life right now that needs to change and it's God's will that it does. God is great at bringing change!

Recently, God was highlighting *where* people were when the supernatural changed their lives. Let's look at a few.

1. Disciples Were Fishing

And as He walked by the Sea of Galilee, He saw Simon and Andrew his brother casting a net into the sea; for they were fishermen. Then Jesus said to them, "Follow Me, and I will make you become fishers of men." They immediately left their nets and followed Him. – Mark 1:16-18

2. Shepherds Were in the Field

Now there were in the same country shepherds living out in the fields, keeping watch over their flock by night. And behold, an angel of the Lord stood before them, and the glory of the Lord shone around them, and they were greatly afraid. Then the angel said to them, "Do not be afraid, for behold, I bring you good tidings of great joy which will be to all people. For there is born to you this day in the city of David a Savior, who is Christ the Lord. – Luke 2:8-11

3. The Samaritan Woman Was Getting Water at the Well

So, He came to a city of Samaria which is called Sychar, near the plot of ground that Jacob gave to his son Joseph. Now Jacob's well was there. Jesus therefore, being wearied from His journey, sat thus by the well. It was about the sixth hour. A woman of Samaria came to draw water. Jesus said to her, "Give Me a drink." – John 4:5-7

What were they doing? They were living their everyday lives doing what they needed to do when the Lord came to them and supernaturally changed things! This is just the New Testament. What about King David, Ruth, and Esther? They were faithful where they were planted, and God showed up! That's what you need to do. Be faithful where you are.

God's word to us:

Prosper where you are planted!

You may be thinking, "You don't know where I am. There is no way I can prosper in this place of my life." You are correct. I don't know where you are, what challenges you are facing, what people are tearing you down, or the weight of responsibility you are carrying. What I do know is this: God is bigger than any circumstance you will ever face. God's presence is the same in *every* situation. You can bear fruit in *every* situation. Sometimes, that fruit is on the outside and circumstances change. Perhaps you do something right and you get rewarded for it. It is fruit everyone can see and celebrate.

Sometimes, the fruit is on the inside. You partner with the Lord and He changes you. Maybe you learn patience, self-control over your thoughts, or you learn how to have peace in the middle of chaos. You may be the only one who sees this fruit, but it's there! It's between you and God. It may not change your circumstances, but it changes you!

And whatever you do, do it heartily, as to the Lord and not to men, knowing that from the Lord you will receive the reward of the inheritance; for you serve the Lord Christ.
– Colossians 3:23-24

But without faith it is impossible to please Him, for he who comes to God must believe that He is, and that He is a rewarder of those who diligently seek Him. – Hebrews 11:6

This is how you can bear fruit in EVERY circumstance. Your hope is in the One who sees everything. He is our rewarder. He sees the times you choose Him. He sees when you change diapers, mow the yard, pray for your enemies, and turn the other cheek. You live in an upside-down Kingdom. Leaders serve, the last shall be first, little children are accepted, and rich rulers are denied. The small things are often the big things.

> *Now Jesus sat opposite the treasury and saw how the people put money into the treasury. And many who were rich put in much. Then one poor widow came and threw in two mites, which make a quadrans. So, He called His disciples to Himself and said to them, "Assuredly, I say to you that this poor widow has put in more than all those who have given to the treasury; for they all put in out of their abundance, but she out of her poverty put in all that she had, her whole livelihood." – Mark 12:41-44 (NKJV)*

Do you feel stuck in a business, job, relationship, ministry, family or somewhere else? What if the very places and situations you are trying to wiggle away from are actually the soil God planted you in to prepare you for an upgrade? You can prosper where you are planted *right now,* knowing your loving Heavenly Father will transplant you to a bigger pot when it's time.

God Will Open the Next Door

In my younger days, I was trying to pursue a career in Christian music. I was working on writing songs and trying to get a demo together. During that time, I heard that Darrell Evans was performing and signing CDs at a bookstore. He had several hit songs including "Trading My Sorrows."[21] After the performance, I stood in line to meet him. When I got to him, I said, "What would you tell someone who wants to get into Christian music?" He looked at me and said,

"You are not going to like what I have to say." I thought to myself, "Oh, no! He's prophetic and God told him I wasn't very good, and I should just give up." That was not the case!

He said, "I was sending out demos and doing everything I could to promote myself. Then God said, 'Stop. Love the people in front of you and I will open the next door. Then love the people in front of you and I will open next door. Then love the people in front of you and I will open next door.'"

Wow! That conversation changed my life! It has become the foundation for almost everything I do. It was the best thing he could have told me. Ten years later, I saw him again and thanked him for those words of wisdom. I didn't pursue Christian music, but I have found hope in those words over and over again. You don't need to promote yourself or rely on man. Please be confident and proactive but know God will place you where He wants you.

In every situation, ask, "How can I bring God's love into this?" You'll know when He opens the next door for you. It's not about loving people so the next thing can come. It's staying in the moment while you hope for the future. You will only prosper where you are planted if you grow roots. Those roots are established by LOVE! Water yourself with the Holy Spirit and stay in the light.

Could prospering where we are planted be that simple? Yes.

1) Be faithful where you are and with what you have been given.

2) Love. Receive God's love. Love God, love yourself, and love others.

24

RUN YOUR RACE

am not a runner, but my husband used to be. Many years ago, he coached a marathon team. He would get up at 5 a.m. on Saturday to set up a route for them to train and we would make 50 gallons of Gatorade for them to drink.

It came time for the White Rock Marathon in Dallas and I volunteered to help. I got the humbling job of removing the timing chip off their sweaty shoes after the runners crossed the finish line. This meant I had to bend over at least 1,000 times. Even though I was so sore the next day, I had a blast! It was so awesome to be there and see the excitement as each runner crossed the finish line.

Most people wanted to tell me about their goal. They would say, "I made my goal," or "I missed it by 20 minutes, but I'll get it next time." One told me how he lost a toenail at mile 13. Another got diarrhea and had to stop at the Port-a-Potty at mile 19. Other runners got blisters, shin splint, leg cramps, and they talked about how they wanted to stop at around mile 20 but found the energy to keep going.

Although all these gross things happened to them, they still couldn't contain their excitement. Why weren't they whining and complaining? Because it didn't matter anymore. What mattered was they had finished the race and all of the struggles along the way were things they expected to happen. They had been prepared, forewarned, about these things, so they knew to keep going anyway. They were equipped to run their race and taught to persevere.

We are in a race. The apostle Paul used the word *race* several times when he wrote to describe the Christian life.

The Race of Faith

Therefore we also, since we are surrounded by so great a cloud of witnesses, let us lay aside every weight, and the sin which so easily ensnares us, and let us run with endurance the race that is set before us, looking unto Jesus, the author and finisher of our faith, who for the joy that was set before Him endured the cross, despising the shame, and has sat down at the right hand of the throne of God. – Hebrews 12:1-2

Before I start, I want to make sure you know you don't have to be perfect to make it into heaven. Thank God! You do need to choose the One who is perfect to be your Lord. When you choose Jesus, He chooses you forever. The following life principles only work through a relationship with Jesus. Trying to accomplish these things outside of relationship with Him is only a work of the flesh.

The race of this life is to become more like Jesus day by day. As we do, we have a whole lot less trouble. Our race is also meant to draw others into the Kingdom as we find victory ourselves.

Helpful Tips for Runners:

1. Stay in Your Lane

I have been married 22 years, and there are still times I think I know how to live my husband's life better than he does. There was one particular time I thought I really knew what Kevin needed to be doing and he wasn't. I was frustrated at how his decisions were affecting me and wanted to impose my will on him so life would get better. I can tell you exactly where I was when I heard the Lord talk to me about this.

We had just come back from the gym and the Lord clearly said, "Stay in your lane, Nicole." I had never ever heard that before from anyone, especially not God. It made so much sense to me. I realized I have my own lane and Kevin has his even though we are married. We each have our own lane. We are never called to run someone else's race for them. We are called to run our own and run it well.

Let the Lord lead you regarding "how" to help others, because we often try to help "our" way. Trust the Lord's way for them. His love is perfect and so is His plan. Let Him show you how to pray for others when you see them stumbling in their own lane. That way, we can cheer them on and support them without trying to do it for them.

Trust in the Lord with all your heart, and lean not on your own understanding; In all your ways acknowledge Him, and He shall direct your paths... – Proverbs 3:5-6

Ask the Lord to show you *your* lane. Your lane will affirm your value. It is also a good thing to have healthy boundaries with people so they don't jump in your lane. Shame and condemnation don't belong in anyone's lane. Don't allow them in your lane and don't put them in someone else's lane either.

The truth is, we don't have the grace to handle the hurdles in someone else's life because they are not our hurdles. We have the grace to handle ours. It's also true that if I'm not in my lane running my race, no one is.

2. Run in Your Own Shoes

There will be seasons where you run the race of your life in running shoes but there will also be seasons when you run in bath slippers, hiking boots, and maybe even flip-flops or bare feet. Dress for the occasion but whatever you do, make sure you are running in your *own* shoes. King David knew this. This is what happened right after King Saul gave him permission to face Goliath:

Then Saul dressed David in his own tunic. He put a coat of armor on him and a bronze helmet on his head. David fastened on his sword over the tunic and tried walking around, because he was not used to them. "I cannot go in these," he said to Saul, "because I am not used to them." So, he took them off.

Then he took his staff in his hand, chose five smooth stones from the stream, put them in the pouch of his shepherd's bag and, with his sling in his hand, approached the Philistine.
– 1 Samuel 17:38-40 (NIV)

David could not have done what he was called to do – kill a giant – if he had tried to do it the way Saul did. Sometimes, we are called to do the same thing as someone else, but to do it a different way. My husband and I sometimes work out together. He's a machine, but I am not – yet!

While I'm *modifying the modified version* on the workout video, he's doing extra pull-ups and adding weight. If I tried to work out the way he does, I would feel like a failure. But, God never called me to do that. When God gives you an assignment, make sure you ask Him "how." Discern the season and know what shoes you need, but make sure they are yours. Don't try to be like somebody else. If you do, chances are you won't be a good version of them. Be the best you because we need you to run your race. Know your assignment and what your giftings are. Know what your calling is. Stay in your lane and do what you are supposed to do well.

Why? People are watching, and they need to see our lives as a testimony of God's love. If you are not authentically doing "you" in your own lane, who will fill that role in the kingdom?

3. Keep Your Eyes on Jesus

Paul says we need to "fix" our eyes on Jesus. He is our prize. Eternity with a perfect Savior. Look to Him to find your identity, comfort, strength and direction. You do not see elite runners looking behind or beside them as they run. Why? Because it slows them down.

You don't need to look behind you. Jesus will redeem your past. You don't need to turn around and stare at it as if it is your future.

Here's how it will work: your past will be like a flashback in a movie. When you keep your eyes forward and fixed on Him, He will bring a flashback of redemption into your path. Don't let the weight of your past hold you down. Let it go and keep your eye on the prize. When you do, the redemption of your past will come into your future.

You also don't need to look at others and compare your lives to theirs. Bible stories like Cain and Abel, and Jacob and Esau remind us this never ends well. Like I said, I have been married 22 years. I have two children, Andrew and Jade. We are not big on taking family pictures. When we can get a picture with all of us together, it's a rare treat. The last opportunity we had was at my cousin's wedding.

This mama was happy to have pictures. They turned out so great. Here is the backstory: The first thing Kevin said to me when he walked into the wedding was, "I forgot my belt." Andrew had worn his Nike T-shirt under his white shirt and you could see the logo. My shoes were hurting my feet so I just slipped them on and left them unbuckled.

I had the honor of being the Wedding Coordinator. That meant I needed to stay for the reception. Kevin was going out of town and needed to pack. Before he walked out the door I said, "Wait. Let's get a picture." We left the dinner table and snapped a few shots. If you look closely, as I did when I was making it my profile picture, I still had some dinner in my teeth! Things are not always as great as they seem.

It is such a waste of time to compare our lives to the lives of others. There is just no benefit in it. Comparison kills. It kills friendships, ministries and our self-esteem because too often, we compare ourselves to a standard that isn't even real! Like when I tried different kinds of mascara because I thought my friends had a magic product to create long lashes and then I found out their lashes were fake.

It's also not a good idea to go looking for other people's faults to make yourself feel better. While we can learn and be inspired by people, remember not to fall into the trap of jealousy or comparison. I have a saying: "I want *all* of what God has for me. Not *part* of what He has for someone else."

Rejoice over other people's victories. If you don't, you make their victory into your defeat. That's just crazy! When you see the awesome photos on Facebook, remember that their best day does not have to be your worst.

God has something for you that may not be for them. Keep your eyes on Jesus. It's the best way to ensure you are headed in the right direction at the pace you need to run. The more you learn to fix your eyes on Jesus, the closer you are to Him. The more you know Him, the more comfortable you'll be with who you are in Christ.

4. Run in Freedom

Paul says, "Let us lay aside every weight, and the sin which so easily ensnares us..."

You don't see runners using weights to train on race day. They don't strap on ankle weights to get more resistance to build muscle or hold their hand weights as they're running. That would be crazy! They want to win, and extra weight doesn't help achieve that goal. In fact, they wear the lightest shoes and clothes they can!

There are things in life that may not be bad. In fact, they may be good things, but they have the potential to slow us down or even stop us in our tracks – death, marriage, babies, relationship problems, new jobs, unemployment, divorce, health issues. They can feel like very heavy weights if not handled *with* the Lord and seen through His eyes. It may even be a bunch of little things that have added up to heaviness. We are wise enough to not pick up a huge weight without His help, but little ones can "sneak" in one by one. The weight can feel so heavy, you can barely put one foot in front of the other and it hinders us from what God has called us to be. Jesus says His yoke is easy and His burden is light. We are supposed to cast our cares upon Him. It does no good to hang onto a weight that you can't even handle on your own. He wants us to give Him the weight of our lives and trust His perfect love will carry us through. One of my favorite passages of Scripture is Philippians 4.

> *Rejoice in the Lord always. I will say it again: Rejoice! Let your gentleness be evident to all.*
>
> *The Lord is near. Do not be anxious about anything, but in every situation, by prayer and petition, with thanksgiving, present your requests to God. And the peace of God, which transcends all understanding, will guard your hearts and your minds in Christ Jesus. – Philippians 4:4-7 (NIV)*

Our role is to rejoice in Him, thank Him before the outcome, and cast our cares upon Him. Then His peace will guard our hearts and minds. This means we can have peace when it makes no sense to have peace. We can keep running when we should have been knocked out of the race. This does not mean things won't be hard or hurtful in life. There is a way to persevere through a trial by giving Jesus the weight of it. Then, your actions are empowered by Him and not your own strength. Give Him the weight!

Paul also talks about getting rid of the sin that entangles us. Wouldn't it be crazy to tie our hands together and tie our feet together on race day? Isn't that what sin does? What sin has you entangled – addiction, gossip, unforgiveness, bitterness, offense, infidelity? Remember there is no condemnation for those who are in Christ. So, those sins popping up in your head right now are coming to mind because God has freedom for you, not condemnation. God says we can "lay aside every weight, and the sin which so easily ensnares us." By His power, it is possible. Find your freedom. Let go of the weight and break the entanglements!

5. Have Faith

You need faith to run this race. You need to know what you believe and who you believe in. Don't have faith in your faith. Have faith in the One you believe in. What you believe is your foundation and your support.

> And without faith it is impossible to please God, because anyone who comes to him must believe that he exists and that he rewards those who earnestly seek him. – Hebrews 11:6 (NIV)

Sometimes we forget to understand the context of the scriptures we read. I bet most of you know what comes right before Hebrews 12 – Hebrews 11. This chapter is about incredible people in the Bible who ran the race because they believed in the Lord. Did they do it perfectly? Nope, but they finished their race. They did what they were called to do, and we are still learning from them. Hebrews 12:1 says, "We are surrounded by such a cloud of witnesses..."

They are not mere spectators watching from above. They are witnesses – examples for us to follow. They are people who saw successful outcomes for the Kingdom as they ran their races. They are the inspiration we can use to run our race. They help us realize that even if we're not perfect, it's okay. Keep going. Have faith in God's plan for your life and His power to help you fulfill it.

The people in Hebrews 11 believed God keeps His promises. If your faith is securely in Him and you believe He is who He says He is, and He will do what He says He's going to do, your race is going to be amazing because you know that He rewards you. Not many people are motivated to run a race without a reward. Hebrews 11:6 says what you believe about God is everything. He is a rewarder.

The great thing about this race is we are not competing against one another. We are growing in our relationship with Jesus along the way and becoming more like Him. He is not just waiting for us at the finish line, He is with us as we take each step. He is faithful to help us along the way. He's the best coach ever. Take time to know Him – really know Him.

How Do You Win This Race?

You don't quit. Remember how others had prepared the runners for the White Rock Marathon? I can guarantee that part of their pep talk was not telling them when to quit. Paul encourages us to persevere.

"I press on toward the goal to win the prize for which God has called me heavenward in Christ Jesus." – Philippians 3:14

You have the same Spirit helping you run this race:

1)Stay in Your Lane

2)Run in Your Own Shoes

3)Keep Your Eyes on Jesus

4)Run in Freedom

5)Have Faith

And don't quit!

Your race matters!

Now the Lord is the Spirit, and where the Spirit of the Lord is, there is freedom. – 2 Corinthians 3:17

ENDNOTES

Chapter 2

1 "He Is" – You can listen to this song by doing an online search for "He Is" by Aaron Jeoffrey. It may not be your style but the revelation of Jesus in every book of the Bible is so powerful!

Chapter 3

2 Brewer, Troy A., *Numbers That Preach: Understanding God's Mathematical Lingo*. Aventine Press, 2016.

3 Gray, Bonnie. "Benny Hinn Says He's Guilty of Taking the Prosperity Gospel Outside of What the Bible Teaches." RELEVANT Magazine, 9/4/2019, relevantmagazine.com

4 Donnelly, Jenny L. *Still: 7 Ways to Find Calm in the Chaos*, Revell, 2020, p.66.

Chapter 4

5 Cooke, Graham. *Developing Your Prophetic Gifting*. Chosen Books, 2003.

Chapter 6

6 Johnson, Bill "Listen to God's Voice Alone" Sermons 2019, YouTube.

7 McGee, Robert S., and Jack Crabtree. *The Search for Significance*. Thomas Nelson, 2003.

Chapter 7

8 Maxwell, John C. *Leadership 101*. Thomas Nelson, 2002.

9 "The Coming King Foundation" Prayer Garden, Kerrville, Texas. http://www.thecomingkingfoundation.org/

Chapter 11

10 Michaels, Jillian. *Unlimited: a Three-Step Plan for Achieving Your Dreams*. Three Rivers Press, 2012.

Chapter 13

11 Hayford, Jack W., et al. *New Spirit-Filled Life Bible*. Thomas Nelson, 2015.

Chapter 14

12 Wilkinson, Bruce, et al. *The Dream Giver*. Multnomah Publishers, 2003.

Chapter 15

13 Kung Fu Panda, directed by Mark Osborne and John Stevenson, DreamWorks Animation, 2008.

14 Dictionary.com and Wikipedia.org used for word definitions.

Chapter 17

15 Hagee, John, "Meekness is Not Weakness; It Is the Power Under Control," July 24, 2018.

Chapter 18

16 Burk, Arthur "The Spirit of Jealousy," Plumbline Ministries, 2002.

Chapter 19

17 Frost, Jack and Trisha. "Shiloh Place Ministries Home." Shiloh Place Ministries Home, www.shilohplace.org/.

Chapter 20

18 Niebuhr, Reinhold "The Serenity Prayer" adapted by Alcoholics Anonymous.

19 We Bought a Zoo, directed by Cameron Crowe, 20th Century Fox, 2011.

Chapter 21

20 Eldredge, Stasi. Becoming Myself: Embracing God's Dream of You. David C Cook, 2014.

Chapter 23

21 "Trading My Sorrows" – You can listen to this song by doing an online search for "Trading My Sorrows" by Darrell Evans.

Troy Brewer (a.k.a. Pastor Troy) quotes from various sermons at OpenDoor Church in Burleson, Texas.

Connect with Nicole:

 AnchoredinFreedom.com

 DynamicHarvest.com

 Anchored in Freedom

 anchoredinfreedom